ay Canter

Show-Stopping Sport Compacts

Published by

700 East State Street • Iola, WI 54990-0001
715-445-2214 • 888-457-2873

Our toll-free number to place an order or obtain a free catalog is (800) 258-0929.

Library of Congress Catalog Number: 2005924820
ISBN: 0-89689-253-0

Designed by Jamie Griffin
Edited by Brian Earnest

Printed in United States of America

To my number one fans: Poppi and Rae, my family, Monica, and everyone else who has supported my obsession for motorsports and photography throughout the years.

Contents

Introduction

Those who know me and my passion for motor sports should know why I would do a book such as this. I feel that this field guide is an excellent way for newcomers and seasoned veterans to look into the past as well as the future of what is to come for the tuner industry.

Hopefully, we have compiled a great mix of vehicles for everyone. Not only are the JDM people going to like this book, but the racers will have something to look at as well.

There is no right or wrong way to build a car, as long as you're building it the way you like it. That has been the motto of quite a few vehicle builders that have been successful in the tuner industry.

Every vehicle in the book has its own soul and identity and that is what has made this such a great project for me to work on. I worked very hard to construct something I feel that everyone will be able to enjoy and hopefully relate to.

Thank you!!!
— Jay Canter

 2002 Honda Si

2002 **Honda Si**

Sometimes using a car that the general public can relate to is the best way to showcase a company's product. Steve Brown of Alpine Electronics took a 2002 Honda Civic Si and made it into something that takes that idea to the extreme.

While the engine is totally stock, that is the only thing on this track/show car that Brown left alone. He started by converting the car into a center-drive, single-seat car. The only thing that is not Alpine inside the car is the Nitrous Express nitrous bottles used in the doors, Sparco pedals, and Autometer gauges he installed in the "rib cage" of the car. Tons of Type R subwoofers, component speakers, and amplifiers were used to create a one-of-a-kind demo vehicle.

Bottom Line:

Breath-taking, brain-shaking, neighbor-waking, speaker-breaking.

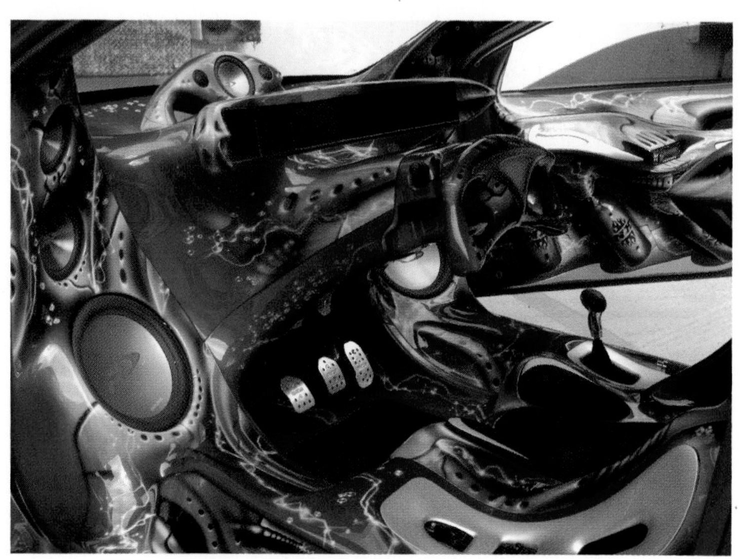

Builder Steve Brown let his imagination run wild inside.

A futuristic sound setup inhabits the back end.

 1995 EG Honda Civic

1995 **EG Honda Civic**

This 1995 Honda Civic CX hatchback street car is owned by Eddie Hahm of Cerritos, California. Hahm replaced the single-cam 1.5-liter engine with a twin-cam 1.8-liter B18C1 engine from an Acura Integra. The engine was balanced and blueprinted, given JDM GSR rods, Integra Type R pistons, and Type R intake manifold, and uses an Erick's Racing 70mm throttle body.

The hatchback uses a Spoon Sports header and Civic Type R muffler. The suspension has Apex'I N1 coilovers, Spoon Sports front and rear strut bars, lower tie bar, and a Skunk 2 rear sway bar. For the wheel selection, Hahm used rare 16 x 7-inch Mugen M7 wheels from Japan and Yokohama Parada tires.

The beautiful paint is PPG Imola Orange mica.

Bottom Line:

All the goods in one wicked little orange package.

The stripped-down interior sports Bride seats and a Sparco steering wheel.

The EG Civic has a hot twin-cam 1.8-liter engine.

1999 Honda Civic

1999 **Honda Civic**

Daniel Song has pretty much done it all to this 1999 Honda Civic Si. He started out with a JDM Bomex body kit, fender flares, and PPG Cobalt Flamboyance paint. He also added JDM Type R headlights, JDM Bomex graphics and APR carbon fiber F3 mirrors.

For engine upgrades, Song started with a supercharger, aftercooler, fuel rail, fuel pump, and fuel pressure regulator, all from Vortech. A Nitrous Express nitrous kit helps add 120 more horsepower. To get the car lower to the ground, Tein SS coilovers were used. 18 x 9.5-inch Racing Hart Type CR rims with Toyo Proxes tires were Daniels choice for rolling stock.

A custom carbon fiber stereo enclosure surrounds the 12-inch Ample Audio subwoofers.

BOTTOM LINE:

Your woman would dump you for this car. No doubt about it.

A JDM Bomex body kit and PPG paint make a great package.

Ample Audio subwoofers fill the trunk.

2003 Honda Si

2003 **Honda Si**

Another APC vehicle to show off the company's newest product. This is a 2003 Honda Si.

On the exterior is an F91 body kit, carbon hatch wing, carbon hood, Retro 3D taillights, Gen 2 LED signal mirrors, and House of Kolor Purple Passion paint.

The 2.0-liter engine was left pretty stock with the exception of an Injen intake and an APC universal muffler. Rolling stock consists of 19-inch ADR GT Sport rims wrapped in Nitto NT-555 tires. Stopping the Si is an SSBC big brake kit. The interior has been redone with custom black and yellow suede seats. Finally, the audio system was completely done by Sony Xplod.

Bottom Line:

If you're gonna go with purple and yellow, you might as well go all out.

Sony Xplod handles the APC Honda audio.

Custom suede seats match the rest of the flashy interior.

1995 Honda Civic Turbo Four-Door

1995 **Honda Civic Turbo Four-Door**

Dan Chueh built this 1995 Honda Civic four-door from stock form into the turbo terror it is now. The 1.8-liter VTEC engine has a slew of parts, starting with ARP rod bolts, Integra Type R camshafts, ported head, Comptech fuel pressure regulator, 370cc fuel injectors, reprogrammed ecu, T3 turbocharger, Tial wastegate, HKS blow-off valve and an Apex'I intercooler.

At only 11 psi, all this made for the Civic to go down the quarter mile at an impressive 13.1 seconds at 105 mph.

Lowering the Honda comes with the help of Tein coilover suspension. Stopping is made easy with Powerslot slotted brake rotors with Hawk pads. The wheel/tire combo has 16-inch Volk TE37 rims mated with Toyo FZ4 tires.

On the interior, the car sports Sparco Speed front seats, JDM rear seat that was recovered in Sparco material, a JDM instrument cluster, and a simple audio system from Pioneer. The exterior has JDM power folding mirrors, headlights, corner lamps, taillights, side markers, side moldings, rear wing, Ferio window covers, and shaved emblems and moldings. The entire car is covered in Desert Silver Metallic paint.

BOTTOM LINE:

Fast and serious-looking. FBI and CIA guys should drive these.

Sparco speed seats work nicely in the understated interior.

The JDM rear seat is wrapped in Sparco cloth.

1997 Honda Civic Coupe

1997 **Honda Civic Coupe**

Dara Sodano definitely owns one of the sickest custom Hondas on the planet. She started with a 1997 Honda Civic EX coupe and added tons of work everywhere.

To the 1.6-liter single-cam engine she added a Greddy turbo kit, blow-off valve, Nitrous Express nitrous kit, custom turbo manifold, Arias rods, STR fuel rail, cam gear and throttle body. For the exterior, Toyota Supra taillights were grafted on, along with Toyota MR2 side vents, shaved door handles, door moldings, a custom hood, and lots of Candy Apple Red paint.

The interior features custom red tweed and off-white vinyl, Autopower four-point roll bar, MOMO steering wheel, shift knob, pedals, and Autometer gauges. To lower the Civic, a custom nitrogen air ride was installed. Two chrome air tanks, four compressors, and a 10-switch control box are on board to control all the side-to-side and pancake action.

The audio system is appropriately sick. It uses an Eclipse in-dash monitor, 12-disk CD changer, Sony Playstation 2, JL Audio component speakers, subwoofer and amplifiers.

BOTTOM LINE:

Radical. Wicked. Red. 'Nuff said.

The wild 1.6-liter engine is packed with aftermarket upgrades.

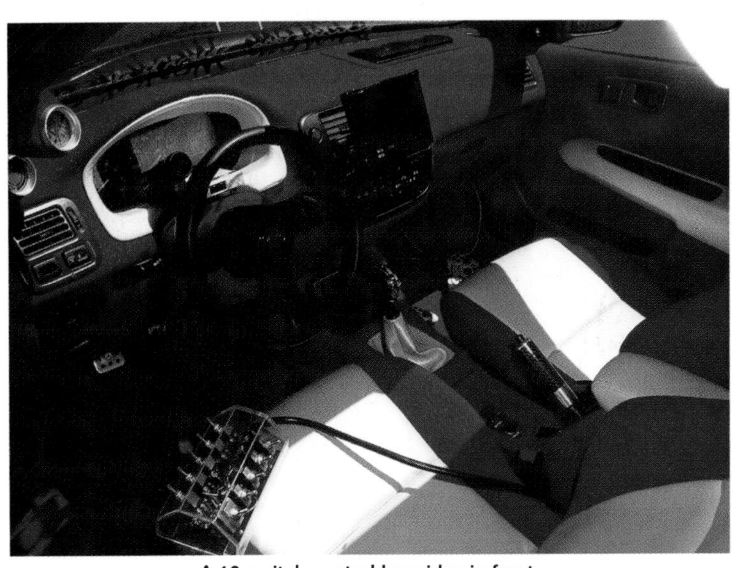

A 10-switch control box rides in front.

 1998 Honda Civic Coupe

1998 **Honda Civic Coupe**

This 1998 Honda Civic coupe built by Wings West sports an Avenger front and rear bumper, Tuner Type 2 side skirts, an Evo series hood and a Commando-style rear spoiler. To finish off the exterior, APC taillights, headlights, euro mirrors, and headlight bulbs were used.

Engine horsepower was increased with the use of a Jackson Racing Supercharger, NOS 50 horsepower kit, DC Sports header, AEM intake, cam gears, pullies and a Sebring Tuning exhaust. Massive 19 x 8-inch Konig Imagine wheels wrapped in BF Goodrich G-Force T/A tires help this Civic roll the streets.

Alpine Electronics installed a head unit, subwoofers, and a six-disc CD changer, while Audiobahn finished the rest of the system with amplifiers, component speakers and TV monitors.

Bottom Line:

Just your basic very cool head-snapping Honda with supercharger, awesome flame paint, TV monitors, sweet wheels and 99 million other things …

A Jackson Racing supercharger tops the list of engine mods.

The nitrous kit packs 50 extra ponies.

2001 Honda Civic Coupe

2001 **Honda Civic Coupe**

Wings West built this 2001 Honda Civic to show its "W" type body kit line. They added Extreme fender flares and hood. Racing Hart 19 x 7-inch C2 evolution rims with Pirelli P7000 tires were used for rollers. In the front, an AEM big brake kit was installed behind the massive 19-inch wheels.

The engine was kept tame with a 50-horsepower Nitrous Express nitrous kit and a Magnaflow Exhaust.

Inside, the Civic has plenty of Autometer gauges, Cobra Daytona racing seats, Toucan Industries strobe and neon lights, pedals, shift knob and e-brake handle. A complete Sony Audio system was installed, including head unit, amps and speakers.

BOTTOM LINE:

You could use it as a really cool daily driver, just make sure you've always got sunglasses on.

Daytona racing seats are part of a very visible interior.

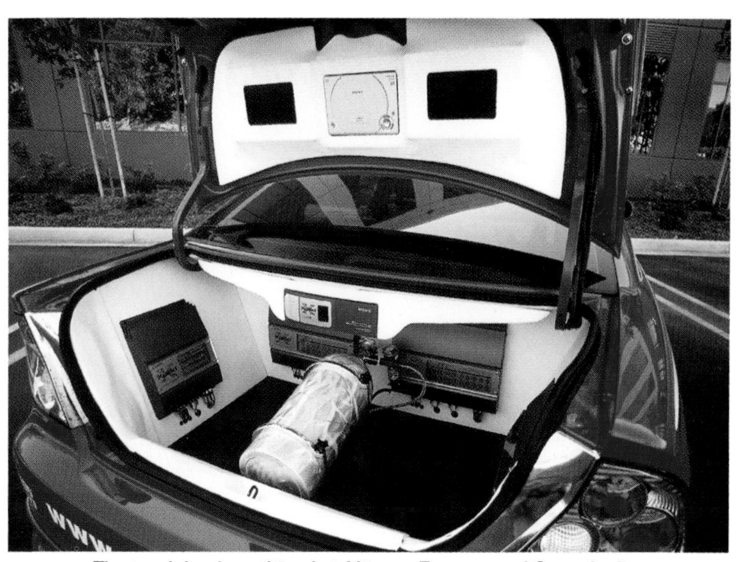

The trunk hauls nothing but Nitrous Express and Sony Audio.

 1993 Honda Civic HB Drag Racer

1993 **Honda Civic HB Drag Racer**

Gary Gardella is the owner and pilot of one of the fastest unibody cars on the planet. His 1993 Honda Civic hatchback has run 8.08 @ 180.66 mph. Running a 1.8-liter twin-cam Honda engine running on methanol and a large Turbonetics turbo, Gardella has been able to produce more than 850 hp.

With an Xtrac sequential transmission, keeping the power on the ground has been no problem.

Learn more about Gardella at www.garygardella.com.

BOTTOM LINE:

Not recommended as the vehicle for your first driver's test.

The one-piece front end aids with weight and accessibility.

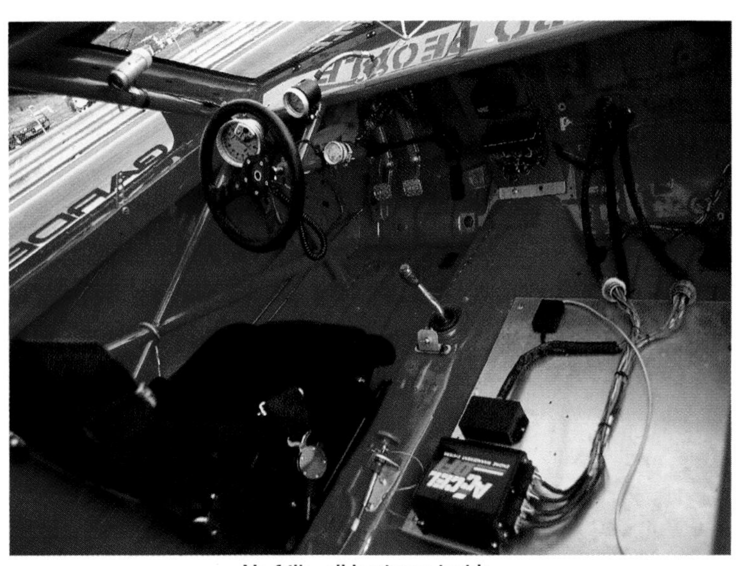

No frills, all business inside.

1999 Civic Chop Top Drag Car

1999 **Civic Chop Top Drag Car**

When it comes to JDM chop top vehicles, Signal Auto is definitely the name that everyone thinks of. Signal Auto took a 1999 Honda Civic hatchback and not only chopped the roof down, it installed a 1996 Honda NSX V-6 engine. The all-motor race car has a 3.0-liter NSX Type R engine with Toda camshafts, pistons, valve springs, custom intake manifold, and TWM individual throttle bodies.

Performance wise, the Civic makes around 300 hp and 210 lbs.-ft. of torque. Signal Auto installed Tanabe Sustec GF201 coilover suspension and other custom suspension stiffening parts to help the Honda launch and get down the drag strip. Goodyear drag slicks cover 15 x 7.5-inch Volk Racing TE-37 rims.

The interior is all business: Bride racing seat, Simpson race harness, Autometer tachometer, and custom fabricated roll cage.

BOTTOM LINE:

A wind-cheating, chopped-top, right-handed rocket.

A custom roll cage protects a bare-bones interior.

The Honda V-6 turns out 300 hp.

1992 Honda Civic Hatchback Drag Car

1995 Honda Del Sol Drag Car

1992 **Honda Civic Hatchback Drag Car**

Andrew Bermea of Deep Stage Motorsports located in San Antonio, Texas, owns and operates this 1992 Honda Civic Hot Rod class drag race car. Powered by a B18C1 twin-cam VTEC engine producing more than 700 horsepower, this Civic definitely has a ton of engine work going on.

Some of the power adders are AEBS sleeves, Ross pistons, Crower rods, 75mm throttle body, JG/Edelbrock intake manifold, and a very large turbocharger. To keep Andrew going straight down the track, Mark Williams axles, spool, brakes, and control arms were installed.

The car has run a 9.22-second quarter mile @ 158 mph.

Bottom Line:

Is 1992 old enough to be considered "old school?" If so, this sizzling no-frills drag sled qualifies.

Acura/Honda

A simple cockpit setup is built for speed, not looks.

Wheelie bars and a parachute hint at this car's pedigree.

1995 **Honda Del Sol Drag Car**

The fastest front-wheel-drive drag car in the southern hemisphere is owned and operated by Online Performance in Sydney, Australia.

Jim and Deni Veselinovic took a 1995 Honda Del Sol and created a tube chassis terror with one of the wildest front ends in existence. They started with a 2.2-liter engine from a twin-cam VTEC Prelude. JE pistons, Darton sleeves, Crower rods, cams, AEM cam gears, Greddy T88 turbocharger, Type R blow-off valve, HKS wastegate, and custom Plazmaman custom turbo manifold.

The engine has been flipped onto its side to create a lower center of gravity. The drivetrain uses a factory Prelude five-speed gearbox with an OS Giken twin plate clutch, flywheel, and a Pro Drive spool.

There is no suspension in the front as it is locked in place. The rear uses an independent custom setup using Koni shocks, and H&R coils.

To date the Del Sol has run a 9.07 @ 158 mph.

Bottom Line:

This Aussie wild thing is the real deal. Pray he's not in your bracket.

The interior features a Sparco wheel and Kirkey seat.

This Honda required some creative bodywork to make room for the huge slicks.

2004 Honda Civic Pro RWD Drag Car

2004 **Honda Civic Pro RWD Drag Car**

The AEM Honda Civic is piloted by Stephan Papadakis. Papadakis holds tons of records including: first Honda to run a 9-second pass; first Honda to run an 8-second pass; first FWD to break the 160-, 170-, and 180-mph marks; and fastest ET and mph in a RWD car.

In the 2004 Honda Civic owned by AEM, Papadakis has gone as fast as 211 mph and ran an e.t. of 6.54 seconds.

The Civic runs a 3.0-liter Acura NSX engine with twin Innovative turbochargers. The internals include Weisco pistons, Saenz titanium connecting rods and Crane Cams.

For more information, see www.stephanpapadakis.com.

Bottom Line:

Before you roll up next to this thing, you've got to ask yourself one question: Do I feel lucky? Well, do ya, punk?

This 2004 Civic has dominated on the drag strip.

Loads of Autometer gauges keep the driver informed.

1989 CRX Drag Car

1989 **CRX Drag Car**

Everyone knows that Lisa Kubo is the queen of drag racing. People tend to forget that there is another queen. Leslie Durst is the driver of a 1989 Honda CRX that she races in the All Motor class. Her father is the team owner and pocketbook for the race team.

The engine is a B18B non-VTEC block mated to a B18C head. TWM individual throttle bodies, JG Engine Dynamics cam gears, Web camshafts, CP pistons, Cunningham rods, and a custom Bisimoto header are all found in the engine bay.

All the braking is done through Wilwood discs front and back as there is no parachute yet on the Honda. All the info on the car during the run can be seen on the Motec instrument cluster. A Kirkey seat with Crow race harness keeps Durst safely planted inside the car. Suspension selection includes Nuformz custom rear with Penske shocks.

Durst has taken her CRX as fast as 9.93 @ 134.99 mph.

Bottom Line:

It's a fact of life: There are women who can blow your doors off. Get over it.

Custom headers are part of a radical engine package.

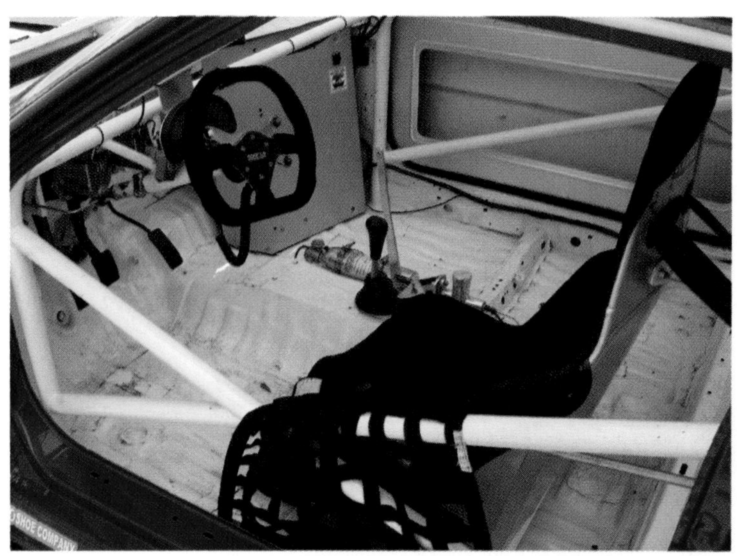

The no-frills cockpit has a Kirkey seat and Crow race harness.

1995 Acura Integra RHD SIR-G Street Car

1995 **Integra RHD SIR-G Street Car**

Greg Leone brought over this 1995 right-hand-drive Honda Integra SIR-G from Japan. He wanted something out of the ordinary as everyone seems to convert their Integras to the Type R front end.

For rollers Greg decided on 17 x 8-inch Mugen MF10 rims with Toyo Proxes RA-1 tires. Wilwood big brakes with four-piston calipers were used to help stop the Integra. Rare and expensive Moton triple adjustable shocks with Eibach springs were installed to help the SIR-G corner.

The engine is the ever-popular LS VTEC with Arias pistons, Crower rods, Web cams, and custom 42mm individual throttle bodies with carbon fiber velocity stacks. For some added kick, Greg installed a Venom Performance VCN-2000 nitrous kit.

BOTTOM LINE:

Could fly in formation with the Blue Angels.

A roll cage signals that this is not your average Acura.

The LS VTEC mill hides under the hood.

1994 Acura Integra Widebody Street Car

1994 Acura Integra Widebody Street Car

One of the easiest ways to get your car noticed is to do something wild to the exterior. Scott King from Speed Addicts C.C. took a 1994 Acura Integra GSR and had a full metal custom widebody grafted onto the body. The body kit uses a Mugen front bumper, VIS Extreme sideskirts, Buddy Club rear bumper and a JDM front end conversion. The Integra was then sprayed with House of Kolor Sunrise Pearl before some ghost graphics were applied.

The 1.8-liter VTEC engine has a ported and polished head, Comptech header, and a Nitrous Express nitrous kit. To lower the widebody, King used Ground Control coilover suspension with Neuspeed strut braces, SPC camber kit and Skunk 2 adjustable upper control arms. Nineteen-inch Velox VX-5 rims with Toyo tires were installed to fill the wheel wells.

Momo seats, Top Power steering wheel, Autometer gauges and Razo shift knob were all installed to set off the interior. The clean audio system uses an Alpine in-dash monitor, 12-disc CD changer, Soundstream amplifiers, and Sony component speakers.

BOTTOM LINE:

An Acura with a distinctly Type-A personality.

The 1.8-liter engine is polished and ported.

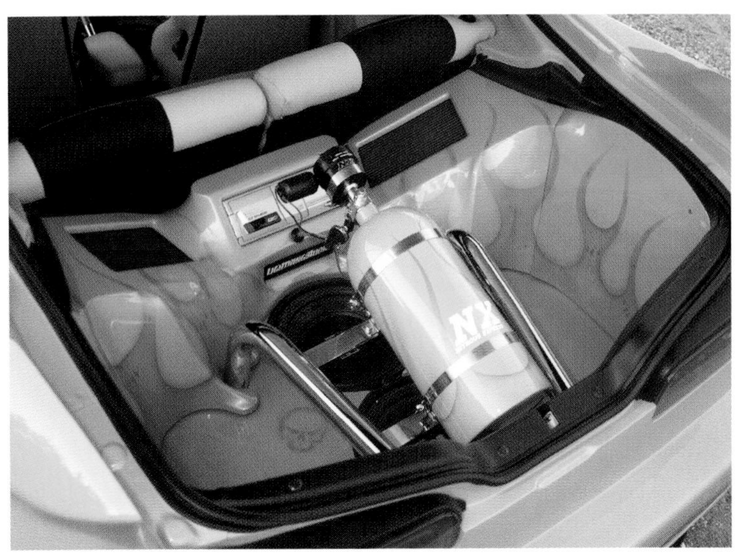

The nitrous is no secret in this Integra.

1997 Acura Integra Type R DC2 RHD Street Car

1997 **Integra Type R DC2 RHD Street Car**

Brandon Bacio from Westminster, California, owns this right-hand drive 1997 Honda Integra Type R from Japan. The exterior of the car is totally factory straight from Japan sporting Championship White paint. The carbon fiber hood comes from Spoon Sports.

The rims are factory 15-inch five-lug models with Yokohama Advan AO32R tires. Shocks and springs come from Showa. Spoon Sports tower and tie bars and Spoon Urethane bushings complete the suspension.

Bacio installed a Spoon Sports air filter, 70mm throttle body, camshafts, and rebuilt short block. The valvetrain is completely Mugen. A Feel's exhaust manifold and exhaust system help aid in the expulsion of exhaust gases.

For more information on this car, see www.inlinefour.com

BOTTOM LINE:

A carbon fiber hood is just the right touch for this understated gem.

The power train includes hot cam, valves, throttle and exhaust.

The right-hand drive helps make this car unique in the U.S.

1998 Acura Integra Four-Door Street Car

1998 **Acura Integra Four-Door Street Car**

Thomas Pinai took a 1998 Acura Integra four-door and gave it a nice JDM twist. He converted the front end to a JDM Integra Type R front-end setup with a C-West front bumper and carbon fiber hood.

To create more power out of the B18C1 engine, Pinai installed a Turbonetics T3/T04 turbocharger, Blitz blow-off valve, STR fuel rail, AEM cam gears, and a 65mm Integra Type R throttle body.

The Integra rolls on 18-inch Roja Formula 7 rims with 215/35/18 Toyo Proxes tires. To go along with the wheels and tires, a Type R five-lug conversion has been performed.

The interior consists of Sparco Torino seats, Apex'I electronics and Autometer gauges. To listen to his favorite tunes, Pinai installed an Eclipse Audio head unit with Eclipse Audio subwoofers, JL Audio amplifiers and Boston Accoustics component speakers.

BOTTOM LINE:

This thing's gotta be a chick magnet. No doubt about it.

Eclipse subwoofers and the nitrous system are mounted in back.

A turbocharger adds even more pop to the B18C1 engine.

2002 Acura RSX DC5 RHD Street Car

2002 **Acura RSX DC5 RHD Street Car**

This 2002 right-hand drive Integra Type R from Japan is owned by David Lin from Westminster, California. The exterior is totally factory from Japan sporting Championship White paint.

The K20A 2.0-liter engine has been ported and polished, and given a bigger throttle body and Spoon Sports air filter and head gasket.

The RSX rolls on 17-inch Volk CE28N rims wrapped in Advan DNA tires. Lin also installed big Brembo brakes. Interior upgrades come by way of a Mugen G-360 steering wheel, shift knob, pedals, rear tower bar, Bride seat and Takata race harness. The audio system is JDM stock from Gathers.

Bottom Line:

A nice variety of upgrades make for another mighty little righty.

Aside from the graphics, the exterior is stock.

Much of the car's custom work is found inside.

1999 Honda Prelude Street Car

1999 Honda Prelude Street Car

This 1999 Honda Prelude was built by Wings West as a demo vehicle to show off the company's Avenger body kit line. WW added a Commando rear spoiler with carbon fiber center and an EVO series hood.

Wheels are 19 x 8-inch Konig Tantrum wrapped in Toyo Proxes FZ4 tires. An AEM cross-drilled and slotted big brake rotor kit was installed to help show off the massive eye-catching wheels.

Engine accessories include AEM cam gears, pullies, cold air intake, a Magnaflow exhaust, and a DC Sports header. Added power comes from a 75-horsepower Nitrous Express nitrous kit. All of the audio system, from the head unit to the speakers, comes from Alpine Audio.

Autometer gauges, carbon fiber and an in-dash monitor adorn the Honda's interior.

The 75-hp nitrous kit livens up the VTEC engine.

2000 Honda S2000 Street Car

2000 **Honda S2000 Street Car**

Clean and simple is the best way to describe Ben Vanderhule's 2000 Honda S2000. The 2.0-liter engine was juiced up using an Arc intake box, intake chamber, and Spoon Sports ECU, headers and exhaust.

Vanderhule had 18-inch Work Meister S2 wheels wrapped with Toyo T1S tires. Lowering of the S2000 comes courtesy of Spoon Sports coilovers. To help stop the roadster, Project Mu SER pro brakes were installed.

The interior of the Honda has a Mugen steering wheel, JDM flat panel 6.5-inch monitor, and a JDM center console. There were many different parts for the body, including a Top Secret front end, carbon fiber hood, C-West side skirts, Feel's rear lip, and a Mugen carbon fiber hardtop roof.

BOTTOM LINE:

Who needs a Porsche 911 when there are cars like this in the world?

An ARC intake setup makes a quick engine even quicker.

The ultra-cool Mungen hardtop is made of carbon fiber.

2002 S2000 Track Car

2002 **S2000 Track Car**

Everyone who is into Hondas should know the name Spoon Sports. This is the legit Spoon Sports Honda S2000 from Japan.

The F20C1 2.0-liter engine sports a balanced and blueprinted Spoon engine, high-rev valve springs, camshafts, radiator, oil pan, carbon fiber intake, header, throttle body and tuned ECU.

The raced-out cockpit sports a Momo steering wheel, Defi gauges, Spoon Sports carbon fiber seat, custom roll cage, and no stereo so you can hear the 9000-plus rpm redline motor scream.

To keep the Honda planted to the track, Spoon Sports coilovers, control arms, and rear trailing links were all installed. Rolling stock comes in the form of 16-inch Work racing rims mated to Yokohama Advan tires. Behind the wheels are a set of Spoon Sports brake rotors and calipers.

BOTTOM LINE:

Tough choice: your right arm, or this car … right arm, this car … hmm… Tough call.

The S2000 breathes through a custom exhaust setup.

A Momo steering wheel and Defi gauges greet the driver.

1992 Acura NSX Widebody Street Car

1992 **Acura NSX Widebody Street Car**

Duke Tubtim took this 1992 Acura NSX and built a 2002 NSX widebody. It took many different JDM parts to create the beautiful one-off machine.

Tubtim took the headlights and taillights off of a 2002 NSX and had them installed into the 1992 body. The C30A V-6 engine has been upgraded with a Comptech supercharger, fuel rails, headers, carbon fiber air intake, and a Gruppe M Style 2 duel tip exhaust. All those parts make for over 430 hp.

To stop the NSX, Tubtim had AP Racing four-piston calipers with 13-inch slotted rotors installed. Rolling stock consists of 17 x 7.5 Blitz Technospeed Z1 rims in the front and 18 x 10s in the rear. The rims are wrapped in Pirelli P7000 tires. To help lower the car to the ground, Tein RA coilovers were installed. Audio components come from Alpine, McIntosh, and Image Dynamics.

BOTTOM LINE:

Can you really turn an Acura into a Ferrari? Apparently you can.

A classy interior matches the rest of this awesome NSX.

The upgraded C30A V-6 churns out 430 hp.

2001 Honda NSX Drag Car

2001 **Honda NSX Drag Car**

Adam Saruwatari pilots a 2001 Acura NSX tube frame drag car. The body is entirely made up of carbon fiber and chromoly.

The NSX runs a 3.2-liter twin turbocharged engine making more than 1,000 hp. Along with twin turbochargers, the interior of the engine consists of Weisco pistons and Saenz connecting rods. The engine also runs a custom-built Hogan's Intake manifold. Stopping power is aided by Lamb carbon fiber components in both the front and rear of the car.

Adam has piloted his NSX to a quarter-mile time of 7.95 seconds.

Bottom Line:

Smoke 'em if you got 'em.

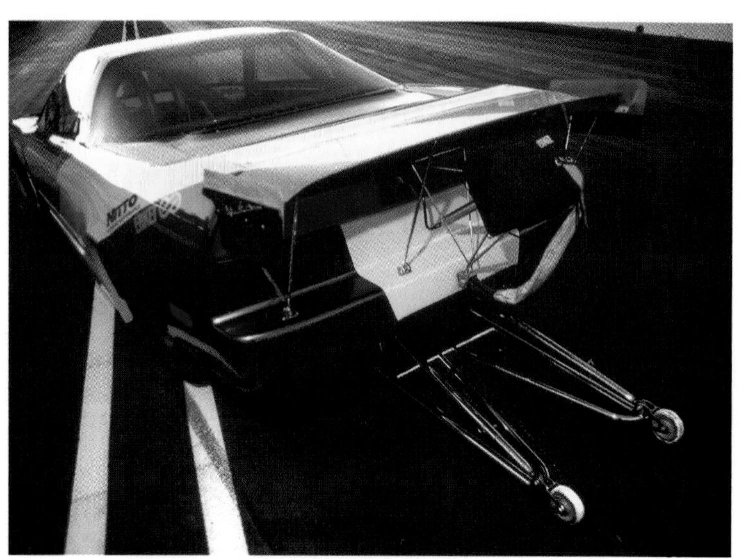

A carbon fiber body keeps this NSX light on its feet.

Twin turbochargers add up to 1,000 hp in this racer.

2005 BMW X5 Show Car

2005 **BMW X5 Show Car**

This is Alpine Electronics' 2005 CES show vehicle. Alpine took a totally stock BMW X5 and created a two-door, two-seat ultimate listening machine.

This vehicle showcases Alpine's top-end equipment, the F#1 Status. With two 10-inch subwoofers, four sets of two way component speaker systems, one set of three way component speakers, six four-channel amplifiers, two digital processors, two 6.5-inch monitors, and a DVD/CD head unit, this is by far the best sound quality vehicle built to date.

On top of the super-clean sounding audio system, this vehicle sports a custom set of 26-inch KMC wheels. To help stop the massive wheels, a set of Brembo Gran Tourismo 15-inch brakes were installed. The interior contains two custom Versus Motorsports seats wrapped in grey leather and suede.

The amazing custom paint on the X5 is courtesy of Noah. He is also the master behind the paint on all the other Alpine custom vehicles.

Bottom Line:

The paint job cost more than your car. The sound system cost more than your house.

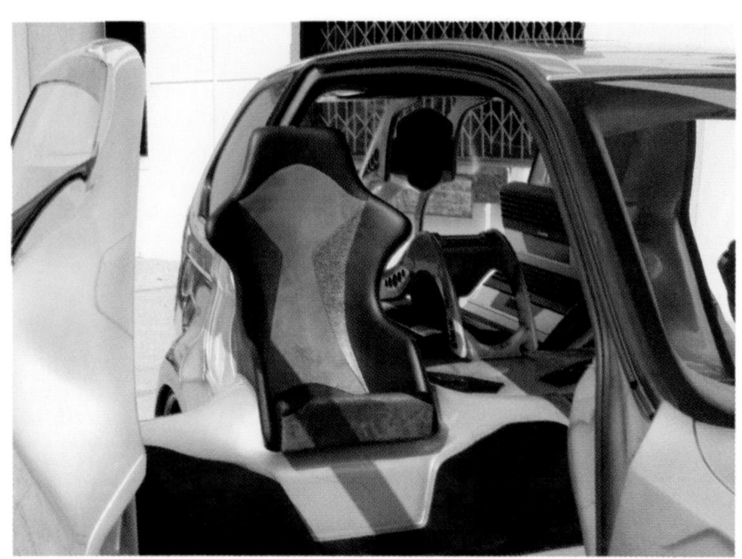

The seat pops out electronically with the push of a buttom.

This insane custom has room for two: one in front, one in back.

2000 BMW M Roadster

2000 **BMW M Roadster**

When Ayumi Wong wanted a new vehicle, she knew who to ask. Les Wong (cover vehicle owner) decided on a 2000 BMW M roadster for his wife. Not only an M roadster, but a Dinan-prepared roadster.

This sporty convertible is a true wolf in sheep's clothing. Able to accelerate from 0 to 60 mph in just 4.8 seconds, the Beemer has a 2.8-liter six-cylinder engine that makes an amazing smog-legal 340 hp and 307 lbs.-ft. of torque. This is achieved through a Vortech supercharger system. Also included under the hood is a Dinan strut tower brace, and a carbon fiber fuel rail and ignition cover. The transmission has been outfitted with a Stage 2 lightweight clutch and 3.38 geared limited-slip differential.

The stock wheels and tires have been scrapped in favor of Work Seeker CX rims measuring 18 x 8.5 inches up front and 18 x 10 inches in the rear. Tires are Michelin Pilot Sport 2 in sizes 225/40 up front and 265/35 in the rear.

The interior was left stock as there is no need to upgrade what is already practically perfect. One unusual thing to notice is the seats in this car do not have the usual M series stitching. Not as cool as the typical colorful stitch job, yet extremely rare by any measure.

Bottom Line:

German chic. Would be tons of fun on the Autobahn.

The BMW's stock interior needs no help.

A Vortech supercharger milks 340 horses from the BMW's V-6.

Mini Cooper Track/Show Car

Alpine Cooper Track/Show Car

Once again Alpine Electronics has built one of the craziest show vehicles ever. This is a Mini Cooper that has been under a serious knife.

For starters the roof was cut off, the doors were welded shut, and a super custom one-off widebody was installed. For the exterior, Noah was called in to paint up the Mini in typical spectacular fashion. The rims installed are OZ Superleggera III and measure a massive 20 x 8 inches in the front and 20 x 10 inches in the rear. They are wrapped in Toyo T1-S tires.

Alpine again opted for the single-seat configuration inside. With a push of a button the rear of the car slides out so you can climb inside. In addition to holding the custom seat, the rear sliding area is the subwoofer enclosure.

The audio setup used for this vehicle is extensive: two 12-inch subwoofers, five sets of 5.25-inch two-way components speaker systems, four sets of 6.5-inch mid-bass speakers, six amplifiers, six-disc DVD changer, DVD player, and seven TVs were all used to create a one-of-a-kind vehicle.

Bottom Line:

Owned and driven by seven-headed space aliens.

Alpine has assembled a futuristic, one-of-a-kind buggy.

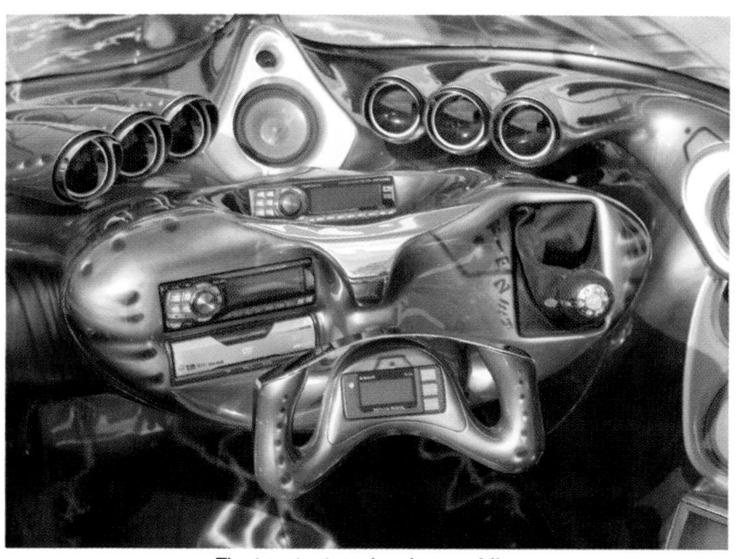

The interior is truly other-worldly.

1997 BMW Drag Car

1997 **BMW Drag Car**

This is one of the most original cars on the planet, thanks to Mohamed "Bar B" from Sydney, Australia. He took this three series BMW, gave it a full tube frame, and put a full custom Mazda 26B twin-turbo rotary engine inside.

There are 16 2,000cc fuel injectors, methonal fuel pumps, custom manifolds, and twin Garret T77 turbochargers. The transmission is an air-shifted five-speed Lenco. It carries an estimated 1,500 hp.

Not only does this car make a ton of horsepower, it also has a full stereo system as well as an in-dash monitor. There is not much time to watch TV going as fast as this car goes. Piloted by Bill Nabhan, the BMW has traveled the quarter-mile in 7.29 @ 191 mph.

For more information, see www.queenstsmash.com.au.

Bottom Line:

Capable of frying retinas while traveling 190 mph.

German styling has given way to drag strip insanity.

The Mazda twin-turbo rotary engine is a work of art itself.

2003 Neon SRT-4 Steet Car

2003 **Neon SRT-4 Street Car**

Built by Street Concepts in Huntington Beach, California, this 2003 Dodge Neon SRT-4 has both looks and performance. The 2.4-liter turbocharged engine has been upgraded with a Mopar Stage 1 chip, Mopar blow-off valve, and Apex'I exhaust. More power is added with the help of a Nitrous Express nitrous system.

This Neon sports carbon fiber fenders, hood, and trunk from GTP. It rolls on 19 x 8-inch Racing Hart Evolution GTS and Toyo Proxes T1-S tires. Stopping force is provided by a big brake upgrade from Stoptech.

The audio system consists of Kicker Audio amplifiers and subwoofers.

Bo and Luke would have no trouble outrunnin' Enos in this sawed-off General Lee.

Suede is everywhere in the interior, even on the Sparco steering wheel.

This Dodge packs lots of carbon fiber and 19-inch wheels.

 2003 Neon SRT-4 Drag Car

2003 **Neon SRT4 Drag Car**

Mike Crawford can say he drives the world's fastest Dodge Neon SRT-4. This Dodge has run 8.26 @ 178.32 mph.

The 2.4-liter engine runs JE pistons, Forward Motion rods, Crane cams, springs, retainers, Turbonetics T-72 turbocharger, wastegate, Spearco air to water intercooler, and a Nitrous Express two-stage nitrous system. The whole works is controlled by a F.A.S.T computer. All this and some top-secret parts make over 850 hp.

Along with all the engine work, the Neon uses a three-speed automatic transmission, B&M Pro ratchet shifter, and Driveshaft Shop upgraded axles.

Inside, a 12-point custom chromoly roll cage, Kirkey aluminum race seat, Crow race harness, Autometer gauges, and a carbon fiber dash. A Strange Engineering coilover suspension is used along with single-piston calipers and dual Wilwood master cylinders.

It's the world's fastest Neon. And it looks cool. Keep your grubby fingers off it.

Wheelie bars and a parachute are essential when you can run 8.26.

The powerhouse 2.4-liter engine makes 850 horses.

2003 Focus Street Car

2003 **Focus Street Car**

APC chose this 2003 Ford Focus ZX5 to help showcase its product line. On the exterior, an APC carbon fiber hood, Gen 2 headlights, Transformer body kit, and clear taillights transform this Focus into a real head turner.

To pump up the 2.0-liter engine, a Gude turbocharger kit was installed along with a Nitrous Express direct port nitrous system. Massive 19-inch Centerline RPM wheels with Yokohama Parada Spec 2 tires were APC's choice of rollers.

The interior received the ultimate treatment. Polk/Momo component speakers, Panasonic head unit, and Audiobahn amplifiers were all used to complete the audio system. The rear seat was scrapped and a single race seat covered in suede was installed. A custom roll cage from Tubalicious adds some race-inspired flare.

BOTTOM LINE:

Impossible to ignore, inside and out.

Custom touches abound in the bright red interior.

A turbo and nitrous setup make this Ford a pocket rocket.

 2000 Focus Street Car

2000 **Focus Street Car**

Wings West wanted to show that even the Ford Focus can be a cool sport compact vehicle. The company took a 2000 ZX3 and installed a complete Wings West Avenger series body kit, a three-piece mid wing and upper roof whale tail. The front half features a carbon fiber hood from NC Carbon, and Hella dual projector headlights. The whole car was painted with House of Colors Tangelo Orange paint.

To lower the Focus, Wings West used H & R coilover suspension, and 19 x 7.5-inch Racing Hart M5 three-piece wheels were wrapped in Pirelli P7000 rubber to give the car an aggressive stance.

To increase power in the ZX3 an F-Max turbo kit was installed, along with a 35-horsepower Nitrous Express kit and a Sebring Tuning cat back exhaust. Cobra Sidewinder seats keep the passengers glued in their seats. Alpine Electronics components were used to make a great sounding audio system.

Bottom Line:

If only old Henry Ford were alive to see this crazy thing.

The engine sports an F-Max turbo, nitrous and Sebring exhaust.

The awesome interior matches the car's body treatment.

 2005 Chevy Cavalier FWD Drag Car

2005 **Chevy Cavalier FWD Drag Car**

Nelson Hoyos pilots this full tube frame 2003 Chevy Cavalier. Hoyos is the 2003 and 2004 NHRA Pro FWD champion. It has posted a 7.40-second quarter mile @ 194.88 mph.

The Cavalier runs a 2.0-liter Chevy ECOTEC engine with a Garrett Turbocharger. The all-aluminum blocked engine produces 1,000-plus hp and more than 650 lbs.-ft. of torque. Redline on the engine is 9,700 rpm. The vehicle weighs in at 1,750 lbs. without Nelson in it.

There are Mickey Thompson tires front and rear.

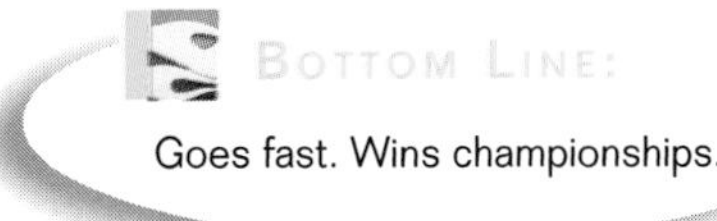

Mickey Thompson rubber brackets the 1,000-hp engine.

This Cavalier drag car is super light and super fast.

2004 Chevy Cavalier RWD Drag Car

2004 **Chevy Cavalier RWD Drag Car**

Owner and driver Matt Hartford from Phoenix, Arizona, has one of the most impressive Pro RWD cars on the drag strip. The 2004 Summit Racing Chevy Cavalier is powered by a 3.5-liter V-6 from a Cadillac CTS. The engine features Garrett GT40 twin turbochargers, Tial wastegates, Fluidyne radiator, Crower billet crankshaft, CP pistons and MGP aluminum rods.

To get the power to the ground a G-Force 2000 five-speed transmission is the choice. Lamb struts and springs are used for the suspension in both the front and rear.

All the go-fast goodies and a heavy foot have been able to get Hartford down the drag strip in 6.61 seconds at over 210 mph.

A 210-mph Cavalier!!? Truth is stranger than fiction.

The Chevy cockpit is built strictly for speed.

Summit Racing has assembled an awesome FWD performer.

2003 Pontiac Sunfire Hot Rod/Drag Car

2003 **Pontiac Sunfire Hot Rod/Drag Car**

Marty Ladwig pilots this 2003 drag racer. The Sunfire is powered by a 2.0-liter Chevy ECOTEC engine. This all-aluminum-blocked mill makes more than 1,000 hp and 650 lbs.-ft. of torque using a single Garrett Turbocharger and running on methanol.

A Hydra Matic 4T65E four-speed automatic transmission gets the power to the ground with the help of Mickey Thompson slicks.

Without Marty in the Sunfire the vehicle weighs in at 2,000 lbs. One-thousand horses and only 2,000 lbs. will get you 7.91 seconds @ 184.85 mph in this radical rocket ship.

For more information, see www.ladwigracing.com.

Make sure you take the wheelie bar off before you try to close the garage door.

With only racing essentials aboard, this car weighs just 2,000 lbs.

A lengthy drag bar adds stability and balance.

2004 Pontiac Sunfire Hot Rod/Drag Car

2004 **Pontiac Sunfire Hot Rod/Drag Car**

Garrett Turbochargers came out of nowhere the end of the season with a 2004 Pontiac Sunfire powered by a 2.0-liter ECOTEC engine running a GT42R ball bearing turbo.

Ron Lummus piloted this rocket to a 7.88 @ 188.70-mph pass. That is the current record for unibody front-wheel-drive vehicles.

For more information on this car, see: www.turbobygarrett.com.

BOTTOM LINE:

This thing goes as good as it looks. And that's saying a mouthful.

This car was the 2003-04 IDRC Outlaw Class national runnerup.

Autometer gauges and a Mark Williams steering wheel help pilot this machine.

2004 Saturn Ion Street Car

2004 **Saturn Ion Street Car**

APC took this 2003 Saturn Ion and showed everybody that you can make any car cool. APC started off with a four-piece Xenon body kit, APC Gen 2 LED turn signal mirrors, custom graphics and paint, and air-ride suspension. The stock seats were covered in black leather with gray suede inserts.

The Ion rolls on 19-inch chrome W64 APC rims wrapped in Pirelli P7000 rubber.

The engine was left totally stock with the exception of a pair of APC stainless-steel universal mufflers.

The audio system uses a Visonik in-dash monitor, six-disc DVD/CD changer, and LCD screens in the headrests, amplifiers and subwoofer.

Bottom Line:

It's gotta be the only Saturn on the block with mind-boggling electronics and playing cards spewing out of the fenders.

Wild grapics and 19-inch APC rims scream for attention.

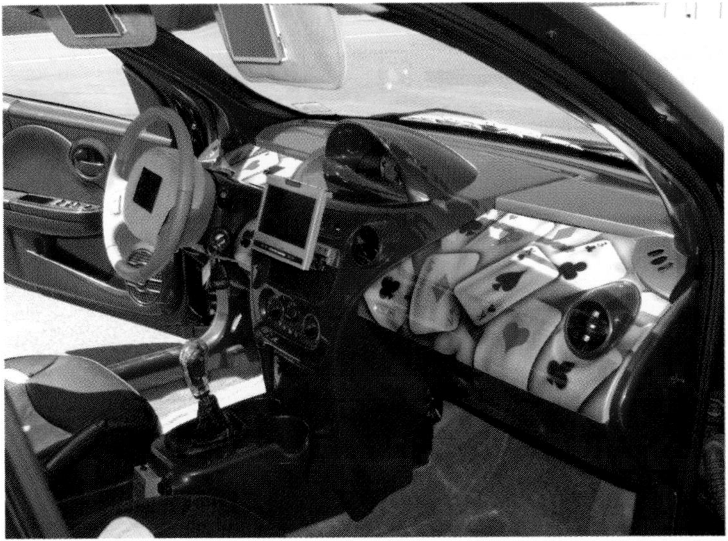

The playing-card theme carries over in the high-tech interior.

2003 Ion Quad Coupe Drag Car

2003 **Ion Quad Coupe Drag Car**

Saturn Motorsports of San Diego owns this Pro FWD Saturn Ion Quad Coupe. It is piloted by Lisa Kubo, the fastest woman driver in Sport Compact history.

Kubo was the first driver to break the 7-second barrier in a FWD, the first female to hold a competition license, and is the holder of numerous Sport Compact Championships. She has run a staggering 7.78 @ 196.76 mph.

Powering the Saturn is a 2.2-liter ECOTEC making more than 950 hp. The block was rebuilt by Golden Eagle. Crower crankshaft and rods and CP Pistons were installed to complete the bottom end.

Boost is supplied by a custom T76 Turbonetics turbocharger. Fuel is delivered by way of 1,600cc RC injectors and a Waterman fuel pump. Lamp Components carbon front and rear brakes were installed to help stop this FWD beast.

For more information see www.saturnmotorsports.com.

BOTTOM LINE:

Just your average, garden variety, technicolor, record-breaking, 196-mph Saturn driven by the queen of the sport compact drag racing world.

More than 950 horses are stuffed into this Ion's front end.

This racer has been made as low and lean as possible.

 1993 RX7 Street Car

1993 **RX7 Street Car**

Les Wong from Elk Grove, California, has probably the wildest JDM Mazda RX7 in the country. The 1993 R1 RX7 has a 13B engine with an Apex'I Isamu RX6 turbocharger kit, wastegate, GT bleed tank, exhaust manifold, custom drift V mount intercooler by Signal Auto, 800cc RC Engineering fuel injectors, and a Tanabe Medallion titanium exhaust.

Along with the beefed-up suspension, 18 x 8.5-inch Work Termist S1C rims were mounted on the front and massive 18 x 11.5-inchers bolted to the rear. Michelin Pilot sport tires are the rubber of choice.

Interior components include Zeal race seats, Takata race harnesses, RE Amemiya Steering wheel and Apex'I gauges. Kenwood, Kicker and Sony audio equipment was all used to create a clean audio system.

Wong had the majority of the exterior parts brought over special just for his car. Run Racing hood and headlight conversion, Apex'I front bumper, RE Amemiya sideskirts, rear bumper, Pettit Racing rear fender flares, Veilside GT3 wing, and JDM Endless JGTC graphics round out the extravagant exterior.

Bottom Line:

Go ahead, take out a second mortgage and try to build your own. It'll be worth it.

This RX7 is packed with high-end components inside and out.

The spectacular 13B engine is a show-stopper.

Mazda

1993 RX7 Widebody Street Car

1993 **RX7 Widebody Street Car**

Jay Laub is the owner of this wild 1993 Mazda RX7 widebody. The car has won more best of show trophies and has been in more magazines than anything else around.

To create this ultimate show car, Laub started with a wild exterior. Lamborghini doors, R.E. Amemiya JGTC widebody kit, C-West carbon fiber headlights, Scoot hood, Knightsport mirrors and JDM taillights.

The 1.3-liter 13b engine makes 485 hp at the wheels at 18 psi, thanks to a Greddy T78 turbocharger, wastegate, downpipe, blow-off valve, Nitrous Express nitrous kit, and a Magnaflow titanium exhaust.

The interior is just as wild as the exterior with Bride racing seats, Takata race harnesses, Sparco steering wheel and shift knob, and Autometer gauges. To finish things off, a Kenwood in-dash monitor, 10-disc CD changer, JL Audio subwoofers and amplifiers, and LCD monitors in the sun visors create a wild and loud audio system.

BOTTOM LINE:

It's hard to know where to start with a "what's cool" list for this car. Awesome from top to bottom.

Lambo doors fit the exotic look of this RX7.

Gauges and electronics abound in the spectacular interior.

1994 RX7 Street Car

1994 **RX7 Street Car**

Tony Yeh is the owner of this beautiful 1994 Mazda RX7. The first thing that stands out is the PPG Harlequin paint, which is combined with an RE Amemiya front end conversion, rear conversion, side skirts, and the Knightsport mirrors to make for a spectacular exterior.

Yeh also added some serious power. Twin TO4 turbochargers, RC Engineering throttle body, Apex'I N1 exhaust, and 3mm seals supply nearly 530 hp. To hold all that power, an ACT six-puck clutch, KAAZ 1.5-way LSD, and custom final drive gears were installed. Yeh uses 18 x 8.5-inch RE Amemiya AW7 wheels in the front and 18 x 9.5 hoops in the rear wrapped with Pirelli P7000 rubber.

Lowering the RX7 was easy with the use of a Tanabe Sustec SS pro coilover suspension. A Momo Champion steering wheel, Bride seats and Apex'I gauges round out the clean interior. The Pioneer audio system sits in the trunk.

For more information on this car, see www.rxecret7.com.

Classy and sophisticated, in a tear-your-face-off kind of way.

With 530 horses, this Mazda is one hairy sport compact street car.

Sparco harnesses and Bride seats make a cool combination inside.

 1994 RX7 Widebody Street Car

1994 **RX7 Widebody Street Car**

SP Engineering built this super-powered 1994 Mazda RX7. It is propelled by a 13B engine with Greddy intake manifold, HKS GT2835R twin turbochargers, blow-off valve, wastegates, and a custom fuel rail with 850cc primary and two 720cc secondary fuel injectors. This engine setup makes more than 450 hp at the wheels on street boost and pump gas.

To keep the power from slipping, a HKS twin-plate clutch, carbon fiber drive shaft, and R.E. Amemiya differential were intalled.

The exterior sports an R.E. Amemiya widebody kit, rear wing and Scoot hood. It's all painted Lamborghini California orange.

A Tein Circui master RA suspension system and racing rear sway bars do the lowering and stabilizing. Wheels are 18 x 10-inch Kenisis Model 5's up front and massive 18 x 12-inchers on the rear, all wrapped in Pirelli PZero Asimmetrico tires.

The cockpit features R.E. Amemiya seats, a Sparco steering wheel, Cusco roll cage, Greddy gauges and carbon fiber trim.

Cooler than a $2 Slurpee down the front of your shorts.

The widebody kit and rear wing provide a great peformance look.

Greddy gauges and lots of carbon fiber live inside.

1993 RX7 Twin-Turbo Street Car

1993 **RX7 Twin-Turbo Street Car**

Noel Rollon is the owner of this beautiful 1993 twin-turbo Mazda RX7. Rollon used a Greddy intercooler, blow-off valve, downpipe, air intake, and pulleys to upgrade the engine to 370 hp.

Suspension comes by way of Tokico five-way adjustable shocks, Vogtland Lowering springs, Cusco front and rear sway bars, and U joints. Rollon upgraded the brakes by using Hawk Brake pads and Powerslot brake rotors.

A Carbon Creations Carbon fiber hood, carbon fiber fenders, carbon fiber C-West style body kit, Rotora GT wing, and Rotory Extreme carbon fiber JDM headlight kit make up the awesome exterior.

Everything electronic, from the head unit to subwoofers, comes from Kenwood Car Audio.

BOTTOM LINE:

If John Wayne ever had a tuner car, it woulda been like this.

Lambo doors and a huge rear wing complete the exterior.

Kenwood Audio takes up the entire rear of the RX7.

 1995 RX7 Street Car

1995 **RX7 Street Car**

This fantastic 1995 Mazda RX7's PPG Harlequin paint and massive 20-inch Momo wheels make it a true show stopper. Danny Hoang, owner of Cyber Motorsports in Sydney, Australia, is known for having wild show cars. This is no exception.

The 20 x 9-inch Momo Magnum rims wrapped in Pirelli P-Zero tires were the first set in Australia. To lower the Mazda, a Tein HA coilover suspension was installed. Along with the PPG paint, the exterior received Ganador mirrors. The rest of the exterior was left alone to draw attention to the beautiful paint work.

In the engine bay, the 13b motor received an aftermarket GCG GT35R turbocharger, XTR wastegate, Tial wastegate, custom intercooler, and a HKS Super Dragger exhaust. The inside received Recaro SPA Kevlar seats, Momo steering wheel and shift knob, and Defi gauges. The audio system comes complete from Rockford Fosgate.

BOTTOM LINE:

A fabulous jet-propelled, high-tech chameleon from Down Under.

This Mazda's huge 20-inch wheels are hard to overlook.

Rockford Fosgate subwoofers thump beneath the hatch lid.

 1998 RX7 Drag Car

1998 **RX7 Drag Car**

Abel Ibarra is known to many as the "god of rotaries." He is the first one to have a sport compact vehicle inducted into the NHRA Hall of Fame. He has ripped up the quarter mile in 7.12 seconds @ 178 mph in his 1998 Mazda RX7.

This full tube frame car sports a 13B 1.3-liter engine with a massive Garrett Turbocharger. It all runs on methanol.

Since retiring this RX7, Abel has moved into a tube frame Mazda RX8. This new RX8 has gone 6.73 @ 204 mph. Both cars compete in the Pro RWD class.

For more information, see www.flacoracing.com.

BOTTOM LINE:

Big-time car, big-time driver.

Abel Ibarra won many big titles in this full-dress Mazda drag car.

The rotary mill makes this car unique.

Mazda

1973 **Wagon Street Car**

Grant Bradshaw from Sydney, Australia took a 1973 Mazda 1300 and made one of the coolest wagons you can imagine.

The engine is a 12a two-rotor engine with a Garrett TO4 turbocharger. Bradshaw's 12a engine is mated to a Toyota four-speed transmission with a custom made adapter plate. A Ford 9-inch rear end was installed to replace the standard weak Mazda differential. At only 10 psi the Mazda made 320 horsepower at the wheels. For rims Grant chose 15 x 4-inch Centerline Convo Pros in the front. The rear needed to be partially tubbed to fit the massive 15 x 10-inch wheels in the rear. Sound system components used came courtesy of Kenwood and Pioneer.

Don't offer to line 'em up. You'll feel like a dork getting toasted by a little green station wagon from the Nixon years.

A turbocharged rotary engine mates to a four-speed tranny.

The bold green exterior is complemented by neutral gray inside.

2001 MPV Street Car

2001 **MPV Street Car**

So how often do you see a cool minivan? Robert Wilson from Modern Image Signworks took "minivan" and "cool" and was somehow able to get them now in the same sentence.

The 2001 V-6 Mazda MPV has a Mazda Design body kit, and grille. Wilson also had a DG Motorsports Carbon fiber hood and carbon fiber wing put on. The 19 x 8-inch Hagen wheels came from Axis and are wrapped in Yokohama AVS Sport tires. The six-piston calipers are mated to 13-inch rotors installed in front. The rear has four-piston calipers with 12-inch rotors from Wilwood.

The engine was kept stock with the exception of some nice polishing and a Nitrous Express 100-hp direct port kit, and an AEM intake. The interior is full of Cobra Suzuka carbon fiber race seats and a full Pioneer Audio system.

BOTTOM LINE:

Guaranteed to get you and the kids to the soccer game in under 11 seconds.

How many vans have carbon fiber racing seats?

A 100-hp direct-port nitrous kit revs up this family hauler.

1995 Eclipse Street Car

1995 **Eclipse Street Car**

Bozz Performance, located in Union City, California, took this 1995 Mitsubishi Eclipse GSX and made it a full custom using some of the best parts from the United States and Japan. The GSX's engine was pulled out and scrapped for a Mitsubishi EVO 3 engine and transmission from Japan. The engine has been upgraded with HKS 3037s turbocharger, 550cc fuel injectors, 272 cams, wastegate, super sequential blow-off valve, GT front mount intercooler, and a custom exhaust manifold.

All these parts and more add up to make nearly 450 hp at 1.5 bar of boost. Bozz used 18 x 8.5-inch Sparco Viper R wheels and Nitto N-555 tires on the Eclipse. Lowering comes by way of a prototype Bozz Speed five-way dampening adjustable suspension system.

Reclinable Bride Rev seats, Momo Champion steering wheel, Takata race harnesses, and HKS gauges fill out the interior. The small, yet clean, audio system uses components from Pioneer, Rockford Fosgate and MB Quartz.

Bottom Line:

No need for graphics when you've got bright yellow paint, red racing seats and tons of cool performance stuff.

Racing seats and harnesses are part of the custom interior.

The engine was transplanted from an EVO GSX.

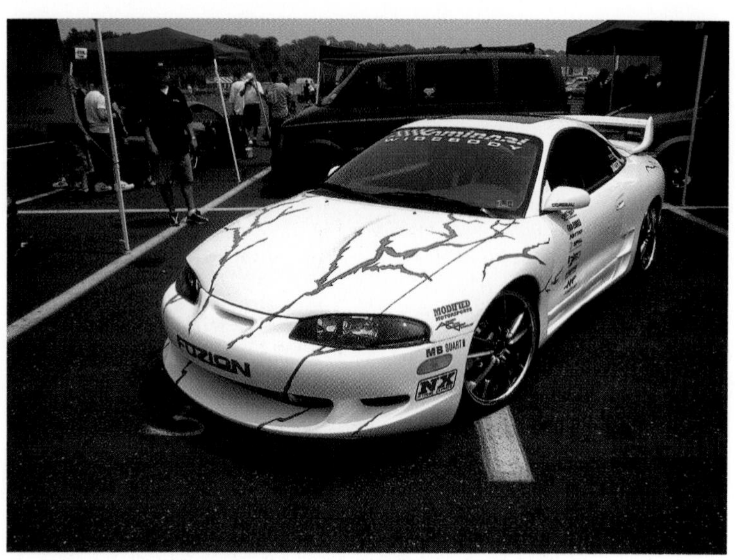

1997 Eclipse Widebody Street Car

1997 **Eclipse Widebody Street Car**

This Mitsusbishi Eclipse is a no-nonsense version of a highly modified street car. It's loaded from head to toe with a 2.0-liter turbocharged engine, Nitrous Express nitrous kit, Injen intake, Thermal R&D exhaust, Apex'I intercooler, RC 550cc fuel injectors, Greddy blow-off valve, and Unorthodox Racing pullies.

A quartet of 19 x 8.5-inch Enkei Phalenx rims with Nitto N-555 tires were used in conjunction with B+G Sport Suspension springs to give the Eclipse its aggressive stance. An HP Racing 14-inch big brake kit was installed to help slow the Eclipse during those high-speed runs around town.

Inside the cockpit are Corbeau Carrera racing seats, Schroth racing harnesses, Momo pedals and shift knob, and a slew of Autometer gauges. Clarion, MB Quartz, and Precision Power audio components were all installed to make the Eclipse sound as good as it looks. The exterior features a Kaminari widebody kit.

White lightning. Woulda made a great bootlegger's car.

Nitrous and high-end sound system components hide in back.

Radical Enkei Phalenx rims cover an HP Racing brake setup.

1997 Eclipse Street Car

1997 **Eclipse Street Car**

There is no doubt that the second-generation Mitsubishi Eclipse was one of the mightiest little street cars ever to come along. John Kargili took his 1997 GST and made a good thing even better.

His engine upgrades to the 2.0-liter turbocharged engine include an Injen intake, Greddy exhaust, blow off-valve, Hahn Racecraft turbocharger upgrade, ACT pressure plate and clutch disc upgrade. Once the engine was finished, Kargili slapped on a set of 18 x 7.5-inch chrome wheels with Nitto 555 tires, Street Weapon front bumper, Blitz side skirts, Wings West spoiler, and Nissan S15 headlights from Japan.

To make the interior as stylish as the outside, the inside was wrapped with black leather, a four-point roll cage, and enough audio to shake and rattle windows across the street. The Eclipse's sound system runs a Pioneer flip-out TV head unit, OZ Audio components speakers, OZ Audio subwoofers, Power Acoustik amplifiers and a Sony Playstation 2.

Bottom Line:

If they took away all your other worldly possessions, but left you this car, you could still lead a happy life.

This 2-liter engine received the full aftermarket treatment.

OZ audio components reside in a stylish hatch area.

2003 Lancer Street Car

2003 **Lancer Street Car**

Robert Wilson of Modern Image Signworks took a not-so-fast 2003 Mitsubishi Lancer and made it a real street terror. He started with a custom turbo kit using a TD04 turbocharger, Greddy blow-off valve, Tial external wastegate, and a Nitrous Express nitrous kit.

To make the Lancer look like its EVO big brother, Robert added a Japanese EVO style body kit. For rolling stock Volk Racing SE37 wheels with Toyo Proxes T1-S tires were mounted. Sparco Milano seats and custom covered rear seats complement the custom roll cage on the interior. The sounds for the Lancer come completely from Pioneer.

Bottom Line:

Plenty of flash, plenty of dash. Pretty sweet all around.

The subwoofers and NX are nicely integrated in back.

Sparco Milano seats highlight the slick interior.

 2002 Lancer Street Car

2002 **Lancer Street Car**

Street Concepts assembled this 2002 Mitsubishi Lancer to show how a nice simple street car should be built. They started out with a NOS nitrous system, Magnaflow exhaust system, and a Rod Millen intake to boost the Lancer's power. For rolling stock, 18 x 7.5-inch Momo Quaser rims wrapped in Toyo tires were installed.

On the exterior, a JDM EVO 8 wing, Ken Style JDM body kit, Twins Custom Concepts front grille, hood vents, APC fog lamps, and graphics from Modern Image were applied.

The interior received a lot of goodies from Momo, including, Street Racer seats, race harnesses, shift knob, shift boot and a Momo EVO 8 steering wheel. All of the audio equipment, including head unit, amplifiers, speakers, and subwoofers, is courtesy of Kenwood Audio.

BOTTOM LINE:

Somebody had the right idea. Automakers should roll 'em out of the assembly lines looking like this.

The JDM wing and body kit are a great combination.

GPS and lots of Kenwood audio stuff is packed inside.

2003 EVO 8 Street Car

2003 **EVO 8 Street Car**

Mike Welch from Road Race Engineering in Santa Fe Springs, California, took an already-fast 2003 Mitsubishi EVO 8 and created something for more than just the streets. At 18 psi, the 2.0-liter 4g63 engine makes 370 hp at the wheels. At 23 psi, it makes 450 hp, and at 32 psi, it makes a virtually non-streetable 520 hp at the wheels.

To create this much power, Welch used a Greddy T67 turbocharger, Type R external wastegate, exhaust manifold, blow-off valve, HKS 272 cams, AEM intake, cam gears, and an RC Engineering throttle body.

To help keep the EVO on the pavement, JIC FLT A-2 coilover suspension, 17 x 8.5-inch Gram Lights 57s wheels and Toyo RA1 tires were all used. Braking forces were increased over stock thanks to front and rear Stoptech brakes. To stay seated in the Mitsubishi Sparco Evo seats with Schroth racing harnesses were installed.

There is no need for any audio system in a car that sounds and goes like this one.

BOTTOM LINE:

Until there is a constitutional amendment, it's street legal.

Road Race Engineering has put together a very extreme EVO.

The turbo 2-liter cranks out a whopping 520 hp.

2004 EVO 8 Street Car

2004 **EVO 8 Street Car**

Owned and operated by Shawn Williams, Street Concepts designs and produces some of the best show vehicles used by some of today's top companies. This Mitsubishi EVO 8 is a great street car example.

With the help of numerous Greddy products, the EVO has been pumped up to more than 300 hp. Four 19-inch Volk LE37 wheels and Toyo Proxes tires were used to make this EVO really handle. The entire body kit is from C-West. Stopping power comes from 14-inch Brembo rotors.

A Pioneer DVD head unit and full audio system from Rockford Fosgate completes the package.

Bottom Line:

EVOs are like the toughest little kid on your block when you were growing up. Nobody messes with 'em, especially one with 300-plus ponies.

Volk wheels and Toyo rubber hug the ground.

Greddy products help coax 300 horses from the motor.

2004 EVO 8 Street Car

2004 **EVO 8 Street Car**

APR built this 2004 Mitsubishi EVO 8 to showcase its new products. The exterior shows off an APR Performance widebody front bumper, carbon fiber wind splitter, carbon fiber canards, widebody front fenders with wheel turbulence exhaust ports, widebody side skirts, carbon fiber Formula GT3 mirrors, widebody rear door and fender combination, carbon fiber GTC-300 wing EVO Spec, widebody drag reduction rear bumper, carbon fiber rear diffuser, JDM EVO VII taillights and a Seibon carbon fiber hood.

The inside is all business sporting an Autopower six-point roll cage, Recaro Pole Position seats, Momo steering wheel, and Autometer gauges. Getting this EVO to handle was easy using Tein Flex coilover suspension, EDFC, APR upper front strut bar, lower front chassis brace, and Hotchkis rear sway bar. Custom 18 x 10.5 Racing Hart CPO-35R wheels with Bridgestone S0-3 rubber plant this Mitsubishi on the ground.

Bottom Line:

Straight out of a video game. A very cool video game.

The interior features a roll cage, Recaro seats and other goodies.

The tail wouldn't be complete without a carbon fiber wing.

2003 EVO 8 Street Car

2003 **EVO 8 Street Car**

Known as one of the best seat manufacturers in the world, Sparco USA wanted to build a car to showcase its products. For this task the company decided on a 2003 EVO 8.

This car is not just for looks. Added to the 4G63 engine are AEM cam gears, Apex'I intercooler, RX6 T76 turbocharger, wastegate, blow-off valve, exhaust manifold, downpipe, and air induction box, a Tomei throttle body, and a ton more goodies.

AAR created a dry carbon fiber hood, trunk, timing belt cover, and spark plug cover for the EVO. Design Craft created a custom eight-point chro moly roll cage to help stiffen up the interior.

Sparco used its own prototype carbon reclinable seats, Lap 5 steering wheel, carbon pedals, easy shift knob, four-point professional race harnesses and SL-C3 sequential led shift light. The entire audio system, from the monitor to the amps and speakers, comes from Pioneer.

It's one of those cars you'd wanna wash and wax every day of your life if it was yours.

The racing seats are Sparco carbon prototypes.

Upgrades are everywhere under the hood of this EVO.

1994 EVO 3 Drag Car

1994 **EVO 3 Drag Car**

The Mitsubishi EVO is better known as a World Rally Championship car. However, Rob Barac from Queensland, Australia, took his 1994 Mitsubishi EVO 3 and turned it into a super-fast street car.

Still utilizing the four-wheel-drive system that came with the car, Rob has been able to get the car to run a 9.97 @ 145 mph on street tires and in full street trim. The 2.0-liter ran that time with the use of a Nitrous Express nitrous system, Weisco Pistons, Billet rods, HKS camshafts, and a Garrett GT35R turbocharger.

Supplying fuel to the engine is done through 1400cc fuel injectors and a SX Fuel pump. Amazingly, the transmission, axles, and brakes are still totally stock.

Bottom Line:

The parachute doesn't come standard, but maybe it should.

The fuel cell, battery and nitrous hide in the trunk.

The interior is part street car, part drag machine.

MOTUL
RUN ME

RVR Street Car

A 450-plus-hp van is ridiculous, right? Not to Colin Wilshire of Queensland, Australia. Wilshire owns what could quite possibly be the fastest and coolest van in the world. This RVR has run the quarter-mile in 11.2 seconds at more than 120 mph!

Wilshire installed a VR4 4G63, 2-liter turbocharged four-wheel-drive engine. To make that much power, CP pistons, billet rods, ported head, billet camshafts, custom turbo manifold, Garrett 20G turbocharger, custom intercooler, custom sheet metal intake manifold, twin fuel rails, 450cc fuel injectors, Apex'I boost controller and Motec ECU were all installed.

To keep the power going to the ground, a Direct Clutch Services twin-plate clutch, four-wheel-drive EVO gearbox, custom drive shafts, and billet flywheel were installed.

King Springs and Koni shocks keep the van low. Rolling stock consists of massive 19 x 8-inch scorch rims with Falken tires.

Everything remains stock inside with the exception of a new steering wheel, Apex'I gauges, custom pedals, and a custom shift knob.

Bottom Line:

Those Aussies. They're all a little whacky.

The fuel system is housed beneath the RVR.

Interior changes were kept relatively modest.

1989 S13 Drift Car

1989 **S13 Drift Car**

This 1989 Nissan S13 was built to compete in the Formula D USA drift series. For starters, Lim had a 2.0-liter SR20DET engine installed. Inside the engine are HKS camshafts, valves, springs, and retainers, a ported head, ARC oil cooler, oil pan, intercooler, and blow-off valve, 850cc Blitz fuel injectors, an Apex'I Power FC computer, Power Enterprise wastegate, and an 1820 turbocharger.

A Gram Light exhaust expels the hot gases. In the drift suspension department, Cusco Comp S coilover, Suspension Techniques anti-sway bar, and Kazama tie rods were all installed. Stopping the S13 is a set of Project Mu B-force brakes in the front and D1 spec in the rear. Gram Light 57s-Pro rims, 18 x 9 inches in the front and 18 x 10's in the back, are mated to Falken Azenus tires are used to get the car sideways, yet under control.

On the inside, a Sparco Pro 2000 seat, four-point harness and a modified Cusco roll cage were all installed with safety in mind. The body has a JDM front end conversion, 25mm-wider front fenders and 30mm-wider rear fenders.

BOTTOM LINE:

This thing could do major damage to your neighbor's lawn.

A modified roll cage protects a high-performance interior.

The turbocharged 2-liter SR20DET engine is power packed.

1996 S14 Street Car

1996 **S14 Street Car**

Non Fujita is the owner of one super sick 1996 Nissan S14. He had large fender flares installed with a Bomex lower front lip spoiler, and a Cusco rear wing. To fill the large wheel wells, Fujita installed 18-inch Advan AVS Model 7 rims with Yokoahama AVS tires.

An S14 HKS Hipermax coilover suspension was added, along with Cusco front strut tower bar, and a Nismo rear strut tower bar. To stop the S14, six-piston Brembo calipers and slotted rotors were used up front, while two-piston calipers with cross drilled rotors were used in the back.

Under the hood is a JDM spec SR20DET engine with Tomei connecting rods, pistons, and camshafts, a Greddy intake manifold, HKS GT2835R turbocharger, intake, and blow-off valve, and a Signal Auto carbon fiber exhaust.

The cockpit sports a six-point Cusco roll cage, HKS gauges, Veilside instrument cluster, detachable steering wheel, Apex'I tachometer and a Greddy shift knob. Finally, the audio system uses a Japanese-only Addzest VRX head unit, Clarion speakers, Kenwood amplifier, and image Dynamics subwoofers.

BOTTOM LINE:

Comes complete with a Swedish supermodel.

HKS gauges and a Veilside cluster decorate the interior.

Big 18-inch wheels roll inside flared fenders.

1995 S14 Street Car

1995 **S14 Street Car**

The Nissan S14 named the "Green Ghost" by owner Badwee Moussa from Sydney, Australia is definitely one of the most creative cars around. Don't let the looks fool you. This car has run a very impressive 10.2-second quarter-mile time.

The engine is a stroked 2.0-liter SR20DET using a T4/T5 Turbonetics turbocharger, NOS nitrous system, Arias pistons, Carillo rods, and Trust camshafts. The transmission is a modified C4 sequential gearbox. The body kit, wing and hood are all custom one-off pieces painted with DuPont Jade Green Prizim and Fire Prizim chromalusion paint.

The Green Ghost rolls on 19 x 9-inch AME rims in the front and 19 x 9.5-inch hoops in the rear. Tires are Pirelli P-Zero.

BOTTOM LINE:

Custom one-off body parts and paralyzing paint make it a one-of-a-kind "Ghost."

Spectular DuPont paint gives this S14 looks to kill.

A plush interior makes this Nissan the complete package.

 1997 240SX Street Car

1997 **240SX Street Car**

Neil Tjin took his stock 1997 S14 240sx and turned it into a super-clean and super-fast street machine. Tjin started by taking the stock body and installing a JDM S15 front end with a carbon fiber hood. He wrapped the top half of the car in carbon fiber to help with the race look. The JDM body kit came from Bomex.

A pair of 19 x 9.5-inch HRE 441 wheels were used up front and massive 19 x 10.5 rollers stand out in back. The HRE rims are wrapped in Toyo T1S tires. To lower the car down to the ground JDM Kei-Office drift coilovers were installed.

To get the 240SX really moving, an S15 engine and drivetrain was installed. A Greddy intake manifold, downpipe, and air filter, Magnaflow titanium exhaust, and a 100-hp direct-port Nitrous Express nitrous kit were all added to pump up the horsepower.

In the cockpit, Nismo race seats with four-point racing harnesses are in place to keep the occupants in their seats. The audio system includes products from Bazooka, Pyle, Lanzar and Stinger.

Bottom Line:

A guy could get in a lot of trouble in this car with very little effort.

The interior has the full complement of cool tuner stuff.

Custom Pyle monitors were built into the trunk lid.

Nissan

1998 200SX Drag Car

1998 **200SX Drag Car**

Mark Ashford owns and pilots this 1998 Nissan 200SX (240SX in the U.S.). This is the fastest four-cylinder car in the southern hemisphere, running an impressive 8.02 @ 170.2 mph—without the aid of nitrous and running mechanical injection.

This dragster is a full tube-frame vehicle sporting an FJ20 2.0-liter engine. Internals include JE pistons and Pauter rods. The T-66 Turbocharger comes from Turbonetics.

The Transmission is a Ford C-4 automatic with an 8,000 stall torque converter. Front and rear Koni Shocks were used, while the rear suspension is a custom four-link with a wishbone locator. The brakes were sourced from Strange and offer four-piston stopping power for both the front and rear.

For more information see www.ashfordracing.com.

BOTTOM LINE:

The owner only takes it out on "Sunday, Sunday, Sunday!!!"

No passengers and no extra weight are allowed inside.

The serious roll cage is not without some nice asthetics.

2000 S15 Draft Car

2000 **S15 Drift Car**

The Kei Office Nissan S15 is one of the crowd favorite drift machines from Japan.

Starting out with a 2000 S15, Yasuyuki Kazama installed a seven-point Cusco roll cage, Kei Office strut brace, Erfolgkei D1 spec coilover suspension, and Nismo suspension links. Six-piston Wilwood calipers mounted to two-piece slotted rotors are used in the front, while R33 Skyline GT-R Brembo brakes are found on the rear. Bridgestone Potenza tires wrap the 18 x 9-inch Prodrive GC-06D forged rims in the front and the 18 x 9.5 rims in the rear.

On the inside of the S15 is a Bride ZETA III seat, Bride BRIX II reclinable seat, Takata race harnesses, Nismo gauge cluster and shift knob, Apex'I gauges and a Venom Performance Nitrous bottle.

The SR20DET engine has numerous upgrades: HKS GT-RS turbocharger, custom manifold, pistons, camshafts, and a Power Enterprise air filter all make its home in the engine bay. To keep the power from getting away from Kazama-san, the Nismo six-speed transmission uses a Nismo GT LSD and a Nismo Super Coppermix clutch. To keep the weight of the car down, fiberglass doors, SARD carbon fiber 3D GT wing, Lexan windows and an M'Sports carbon fiber hood were all installed.

Bottom Line:

Wouldn't it be fun to take this thing and melt some blacktop in the parking lot of your old high school?

The Kei Office drifter features lots of carbon fiber on the outside.

The interior is set up with track gymnastics in mind.

RS·R
13
RECARO

2000 **S15 Drift Car**

Built by Top Secret Japan, this Nissan S15 was assembled with drifting in mind. The 2.0-liter SR20DET engine produces 540 horsepower. The SR engine utilizes a HKS GT30 turbocharger mated to a Top Secret turbo manifold, HKS camshafts, F-CON computer, Top Secret fuel injectors, intake manifold, intercooler, and titanium exhaust. Mated to the engine is a HKS five-speed transmission with Ogura Race twin-plate clutch and a Cusco one-way LSD. Suspension on the Nissan is Top Secret Super Damper Drift SPL series coilover suspension.

Volk GT-C wheels measuring 17 x 9 in the front and 18 x 10 in the rear are the rolling stock of choice here. Mounted on the Volk wheels are Bridgestone Potenza RE01R tires. Stopping the S15 is a set of Brembo F40 calipers with 355mm rotors.

The body of the drift car has Top Secret front bumper, side skirts, carbon fiber GT2 wing, Yashio Factory front fenders, trunk, Vertex rear fenders, and rear bumper.

BOTTOM LINE:

Awesome gold paint, 540 horses, and nimble as a ballet dancer.

It's no problem getting sideways with 540 horses on board.

The 2-liter engine has torque to burn.

1993 Skyline GTR Street Car

1993 **Skyline GTR Street Car**

Steve Mitchell works for Nissan USA so, of course, the only performance car he could imagine owning is a Nissan Skyline. His ride of choice is a U.S.-legal 1993 R32 GTR.

The already-powerful RB26DETT engine was left totally stock internally. Twin Garrett T28 turbochargers, Apex'I air filters, Nismo 600cc fuel injectors, wastegates and downpipes, and an HKS Hiper exhaust were all used to pump up the 280 stock hp.

On the exterior of the R32, Nismo sideskirts, N1 hood lip spoiler and intercooler ducts, and a Glad front lip spoiler provide the street look Mitchell was looking for. The GTR rolls on 18 x 9.5-inch Volk Racing CE28N rims wrapped in BF Goodrich G-Force TA tires.

Nothing needed to be upgraded inside. The factory GTR seats provide more than enough support for any passenger.

Bottom Line:

You probably couldn't get one even if you wanted one.

The RB26DETT engine was given Apex'I filters and a Garrett turbocharger.

A legal GTR is a rare sight on U.S. streets.

1994 Skyline R32 Drag Car

1994 **Skyline R32 Drag Car**

This 1994 Skyline R32 GTR is owned and piloted by Theo Wollett of Brisbane Street Machines in Brisbane, Australia. Currently the fourth-fastest Nissan Skyline in Australia, this car has run 9.75 seconds @ 152.49 mph in the quarter-mile.

Wollett is still running the original 2.6-liter inline six engine with upgraded CP Pistons and billet Crower rods. The cams, head and crankshaft are all still stock from the factory. The R32 runs 1,000cc injectors and three Bosch fuel pumps. Dyno figures are 657 hp @ 8000 rpm boosting 30 psi.

The transmission runs a Quaife spool, billet gears, and chromoly selector forks. Suspension for the GTR is Tein coilovers. The drag strip requires 255/40/17 Federal tires.

For more information, see www.streetmachines.com.au.

Bottom Line:

A lotta factory parts and it still turns out 657 horses. Pretty impressive.

With 657 hp, this Skyline is much faster than it looks.

The 2.6-liter inline six has upgraded pistons and rods.

1994 R32 GTR Drag Car

1994 **R32 GTR Drag Car**

There is no doubt that the Skyline GTR is one of the greatest supercars ever built. The first-generation GTR is known as the R32.

Croydon Wholesalers located in New Zealand has the fastest street tire R32 GTR in the world. Still weighing in at around 3,000 lbs., this car is definitely considered a street car. Pilot Glen Suckling has run the GTR to speeds of 165.99 mph with an elapsed time of 8.55 seconds. On the Dyno, the R32 has seen power numbers creeping over 1,400 hp with more than 1,000 lbs.-ft. of torque.

To keep that power together the 2.6-liter twin Turbonetics turbocharger engine has JE pistons, Carillo rods, and Tomei head parts. To get the power to the ground the GTR runs a Hollinger sequential six-speed transmission with a HKS triple plate clutch.

For more information, see www.croydons.co.nz.

BOTTOM LINE:

Does 1,400 hp void the warranty on street tires?

A pedestrian exterior belies this car's awesome performance.

A mix of stock and racing parts make up a functional cockpit.

1993 Skyline R32 GTR Drag Car

1993 **Skyline R32 GTR Drag Car**

The R32 GTR of Keir Wilson from South Australia would not typically be looked at twice going down the street. What isn't immediately obvious is that Keir's R32 is the third-fastest Skyline in the southern hemisphere.

This true street sleeper GTR has run 8.83 seconds @ 161 mph. Running a stroked 2.6-liter twin-turbo inline six-cylinder engine, the R32 has made over 850 hp at the wheels at only 25psi.

The transmission used is an OS Giken Sequential six-speed from Japan. The clutch and rear LSD is also from OS Giken. The suspension features HKS Drag coilovers.

Bottom Line:

Doesn't show up on enemy radar until it's too late.

All-wheel drive gives the R32 great grip and acceleration.

The twin-turbo inline six produces 850 hp.

1995 Skyline R33 GTR Street Car

1995 **Skyline R33 GTR Street Car**

There is no doubt that a legal Nissan Skyline is one of the hardest vehicles to obtain in the U.S. Henry Chung is one of the lucky few to have such a vehicle. He went to Japan himself to pick up the 1995 R33 GTR from the famous tuner Midori.

The 2.6-liter RB26DETT came out of a N1 R34. With a head built by Midori, HKS 2530 twin turbochargers, oil cooler, Tomei camshafts, Greddy fuel rail, 680cc fuel injectors, charge pipe kit, and ARC intercooler, making more than 500 horsepower was easy. The transmission is a GREX six-speed with dog gears and an HKS twin-plate clutch. Stock wheels and tires were removed in favor of 18 x 10 Volk GT-P rims with Advan A048 tires. Stopping the super car comes by way of Alcon four-pot brakes in the front and V-Spec brakes on the rear.

On the outside, a carbon fiber AB-Flug front lip is mated to a Nismo 400r front bumper, and a Border vented hood was installed.

The cockpit has a Sabelt race seat with Sabelt race harness, Nismo instrument cluster, Do Luck lateral bar, and an Okuyama aluminum roll cage.

Bottom Line:

You'll have to lean across the passenger seat to place your drive-thru order at Taco Bell.

A sleek Nismo wing covers the trunk lid.

Five-hundred horses make this GTR a mean street car.

 1995 Skyline GTR700 Drag Car

1995 **Skyline GTR700 Drag Car**

The GTR700, as named by owner Mario Toborac, makes an amazing 1,350 hp and redlines at 13,000 rpm. This Nissan Skyline R33 has run 8.27 seconds @ 167.76 mph and weighs 2,960 lbs. with driver. It is officially the third-fastest Skyline in the world.

The engine is a 2.6-liter twin GT3540 turbocharged inline six-cylinder engine was created by Jun Japan and is mated to a Hollinger six-speed transmission. Along with a Jun engine it also runs a full Jun suspension.

The fuel system runs three Bosch fuel pumps and six custom 1,750cc fuel injectors.

For more information, see www.exvitermini.com.

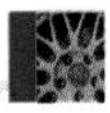

Bottom Line:

A scary purple mutant. 8.27 seconds in the quarter-mile and 1,350 horses from such a civilized-looking racer? That's just ridiculous.

Toborac's GTR 700 requires a hard-core racing interior.

Key items like the nitrous setup, fuel and battery belong in back.

Nissan

1999 Skyline R34 GTR Street Car

1999 **Skyline R34 GTR Street Car**

The Nissan Skyline is a pretty awesome car to begin with, but Craig Lieberman has taken a 1999 Nissan R34 GTR V-Spec and added just about as many parts as you can find to make it bigger, badder, and faster than anything else on the block.

The RB26DETT engine was rebuilt and given a thick head gasket, upgraded pistons and rods, Apex'I IHI-6 turbochargers, 260 cams, 550cc injectors, K&N carbon fiber air intake box, Nitrous Express 150-hp nitrous kit, and a 5 Zigen exhaust.

For the exterior of the R34, Lieberman used a C-West body kit from Japan and had a custom candy blue paint sprayed on the car. Ultra-expensive Ohlins remote reservoir shocks, Goldline Racing springs, 19 x 10-inch HRE 446 rims and Toyo T1S tires were all installed to achieve better handling.

JBL subwoofers, amplifiers, Clarion TVs, and Infinitiy Kappa series speakers were all installed inside.

For a car so loaded on the inside, this Nissan is plenty quick. Lieberman has clocked a 0-to-60-mph time of 3.96 seconds and run a quarter-mile time of 11.75 seconds.

BOTTOM LINE:

Admit it, you'd trade both your parents and every friend you ever had for a car this cool.

No expense was spared inside or out on this great Skyline GTR.

A carbon intake is one of numerous engine modifications.

1999 Skyline R34 GT-T

1999 **Skyline R34 GT-T**

When it comes to Nissan Skylines, people often overlook the possibility of making a cool project car out of the GT-T. Doan Chan of Queensland, Australia, showed how it's done by turning this 1999 R34 GT-T into a show winner and fabulous street machine.

The RB25DETT 2.5-liter engine has been upgraded with a lot of good parts to make the R34 produce more than 375 hp. Rolling stock consists of Exclusive rims measuring 19 x 10 inches in the front and 19 x 11 inches in the rear. The rims are wrapped in Bridgestone rubber.

On the exterior, the most obvious addition is the chameleon paint job. The paint is combined with a Bomex body kit, Ganador aero mirrors, and a front and rear that has been widened by 2 inches.

A super-clean audio install was done with the help of an Alpine head unit, speakers, 12-inch Type S subwoofers, and Soundstream amplifiers. Finishing the interior are a set of Recaro race seats that have been recovered in tan leather, Defi gauges and a C's short shift kit from Japan.

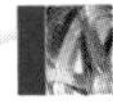

Bottom Line:

This car needs its own TV show.

Big Type S subwoofers gobble up the trunk space.

The widened front end promotes maximum ventilation.

Nissan

2003 350Z Drift Car

2003 **350Z Drift Car**

This 2003 Nissan 350Z track edition car has been set up for drifting. The 3.5-liter V-6 has been taken out and replaced with a 2.0-liter turbocharged engine from Japan. The SR20DET blacktop powerplant makes 402 hp. Lots of HKS, Greddy, and OS Giken goodies make this engine what it is.

Suspension includes Tanabe Sustec Pro coilovers, sway bars, strut bar, camber arms, and traction arms.

To drift you need lots of sets of good rims and tires. Forsberg's 350Z rolls on Volk Racing TE37 rims—19 x 9.5 inches in the front and 19 x 10.5 inches in the rear—with Yokohama AVS Sports tires measuring 245/35/19 up front and 265/30/19 in the rear.

Bottom Line:

Looks like spontaneous combustion could occur at any moment.

The Nissan is powered by a 700-hp RB26DETT Skyline engine.

The 350Z's low, compact body makes it at home on the track.

 2004 350Z Drift Car

2004 **350Z Drift Car**

Built in Japan by Top Secret specifically for drifting, this 2004 Nissan 350Z is powered by a 700-hp RB26DETT Skyline engine. It uses HKS pistons, connecting rods and camshafts, F-Con computer, Top Secret turbo manifold and intake manifold, and a Blitz K5-660R single turbocharger.

Mated to the engine is a Skyline R34 six-speed Getrag transmission with an Ogura Race twin-plate clutch and flywheel. An ARC radiator and intercooler were installed in popular V-Mount fashion to cool the engine and help suck in the cool air.

A Kei Office coilover suspension was used to lower the car. A set of Project Mu six-piston brakes were installed to help slow things down.

The stock body was upgraded with a Top Secret long-nose widebody with one-off front fenders, one-off carbon fiber hatch and doors, and a Top Secret carbon fiber hood.

Bottom Line:

Could easily go 10 over the speed limit sliding sideways down the expressway.

Tires don't last long under this Nissan.

A transplanted Skyline engine puts out 700 hp.

1972 Datsun 510 Street Car

1972 **Datsun 510 Street Car**

Back in the day, the Datsun 510 was a very credible race car. Mario Lozano knew this and took a 1972 Datsun 510 coupe and created a blast from the past.

Lozano started by installing a SR20DET from a Nissan S15. The SR20DET received a full Tomei engine package, HKS air filter, Garrett T28 turbocharger, and a Tial blow-off valve.

To help stop all that power in such a light car, Lozano installed 13-inch Brembo front rotors with four-piston calipers. To go with the brakes, 18 x 7.5-inch Racing Hart C4 rims with Nitto NT-555 tires were mounted.

The interior features a Sparco steering wheel, Recaro RSX seats, Nismo shift knob and a custom roll cage.

BOTTOM LINE:

A worthy update of an underappreciated little gem.

A Tomei engine package and turbo kit make this Datsun move.

Some creativity and imagination made this 510 cool again.

1973 Datsun 510 Street Car

1973 **Datsun 510 Street Car**

Phil Lee took his 1973 Datsun 510 coupe and made upgrades that would make any high-performance vehicle owner proud.

First, Lee dropped in a SR20DET engine out of a Nissan S13. Internally, the SR20 engine has forged pistons, Tomei camshafts and valve springs, Garrett T3/T4 hybrid turbocharger, Tial wastegate, and a custom turbocharger manifold. Thirteen-inch Brembo rotors with four-piston calipers were installed in front, while custom rotors with Wilwood calipers were mounted in back.

Koni coilover suspension, Suspension Techniques front sway bar, and HKS camber plates were all used to make this 510 drive like a race car. To help it handle, 17 x 7-inch Racing Hart Type C rims were placed up front with 17 x 8.5-inchers in the rear. The rims were mounted to Pirelli P-Zero tires.

A Momo steering wheel and shift knob, Sparco seats, Trust race harnesses, and custom roll cage help make the 510 an exciting car to drive every day.

BOTTOM LINE:

Lots of cool new stuff and personality shoehorned into one little retro package.

This gorgeous SR20 engine is far from original equipment.

The remade 510's back seats are a thing of the past.

TOYO TIRES
NX
CUSCO

2003 **WRX Street Car**

With the muscular reputation of the Subaru WRX, Ben Jennings from Quarter Mile Communications knew it was the perfect platform to create a true street machine. Jennings started with the 2.0-liter turbocharged engine and he took an AVO ball bearing turbocharger kit good for 50 hp. Along with the turbocharger, a Cusco turbo manifold, MRT intercooler, Nitrous Express 75 shot, 800cc fuel injectors, and a HKS blow-off valve were added. It all added up to just shy of 400 hp at all four wheels.

On the black exterior Jennings installed a Kaminari carbon fiber hood, UK Prodrive headlights, rear wing, APR carbon fiber mirrors, and ultra-rare Zerosports carbon fiber air ducts.

To help stiffen the Subaru, Cusco front and rear strut tower bars, rear triangle bar, and a custom eight-point roll cage were all added. Ultra-light 18 x 8-inch Prodrive PFF7 rims with Toyo T1S tires keep the car planted around all those high-speed corners. The interior has Sparco Pro 2000 seats, steering wheel, custom rear seats, race harnesses, and enough Sony and Polk Audio to make you go deaf.

Bruce Wayne drives it when the Batmobile is in the shop.

Carbon fiber exterior goodies are among the countless upgrades.

The speakers and nitrous are mounted nicely in back.

www.subaru-sti.co.jp
C-2
NGK
ORTEC
FRAM
TAKATA
Neo Globe
gram
LIGHTS
LIGHT WEIGHT CONCEPT
57
GReddy
sparco
EXEDY
STi
ESPELIR
TOYO TIRES
LIGHTWEIGHTCONCEPT
RAYS

WRX Street Car

This WRX is mild mannered under the hood, but plenty wild on the outside.

The engine features a Greddy Intercooler, blow-off valve and piping, an Injen Intake, AEM pully and Gram Lights exhaust.

Exterior shows off a rare Gram Lights Competition body kit with carbon fiber ducts, GT wing and JDM headlights. It wouldn't be a Gram Lights vehicle be without Gram Lights wheels—17 x 8.5 inch 57s models with Toyo Proxes tires. Behind the wheels are Project Mu rotors and pads. The WRX was lowered with Espelir Springs. Audio comes from a Clarion head unit, JL Audio subwoofer and MB Quartz speakers.

Looks like a pro rally car, but definitely more of a daily driver than a racer.

Decals, body kit and JDM headlights give the WRX lots of flash.

The Gram Lights exhaust helps the WRX exhale.

2002 RHD WRX Street Car

2002 **RHD WRX Street Car**

5 Zigen USA brought over a 2002 Subaru WRX from Japan as a demo vehicle to show the public hardcore products in a street car.

This WRX has a complete body kit from C-West, 18-inch wheels from 5 Zigen and tires from Dunlop. To lower the Subaru, JIC coilovers were installed. The 2-liter engine was upgraded with an ARC front-mount intercooler, upgraded turbocharger, and custom pistons and rods. All together, this combination makes more than 350 hp.

Bride seats with Takata race harnesses highlight the inside. The rear seat is recovered in Bride seat fabric.

An aftermarket parts catalog on wheels. Overflowing with stuff to make you go fast and look good.

A carbon fiber wing and C-West body kit transformed this WRX.

New internals and a turbocharger fortify the engine.

2002 WRX Street Car

2002 **WRX Street Car**

From the moment Shaun Lucero saw the Subaru WRX he knew he had to have one. And once he picked up his 2002 WRX, the first thing he did was have a complete C-West V2 body kit installed. The exterior also sports JDM projector headlights, APR carbon fiber canards and a pair of Zero Sports wing extensions.

To create more horsepower, Lucero knew the only place to take his car was Easy Street Motorsports. Known for its high-horsepower engines, Easy Street installed an ESX 500 engine package. This included an Innovative turbocharger, Tial wastegate, Turbosmart blow-off valve, K&N air filter and lots more goodies. All this was done to get the WRX down the drag strip in a very fast 11.34 seconds.

Lucero decided bigger is better when it comes to wheel selection, and massive 19-inch Arceo Alpinestar wheels with BF Goodrich tires were the rollers of choice.

The audio system includes an Eclipse head unit, Autotek amplifiers, JL Audio subwoofers, and MB Quartz component speakers.

Bottom Line:

Don't pull up next to it at a stoplight and rev your engine, junior. You'll be sorry.

Superb body lines and big 19-inch wheels work great together.

Easy Street Motorsports helped juice up the engine.

2003 WRX Street Car

2003 **WRX Street Car**

Rudi Marci's Subaru WRX has the best of both worlds—hot performance and hot looks. Under the hood is a 2.0-liter turbocharged engine with JE pistons, Eagle rods, Greddy T76 turbocharger upgrade, and a heap of other Greddy performance products.

Marci's WRX has 18 x 7.5-inch Volk Racing SE37 rims with Toyo Proxes RA-1 Tires. The exterior sports JDM projector headlights, STi front grille, STi foglight covers, and a Kaminari carbon fiber hood.

Inside, there is a Cusco six-point roll cage, STi Seats in both the front and rear, STi steering wheel, and Willans Race harnesses. The audio system is completely done with Clarion Audio equipment. Marci added a Playstation 2 for his rear passengers to enjoy on long trips.

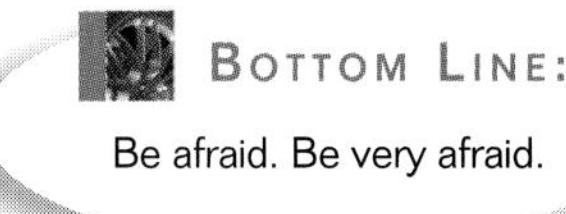

BOTTOM LINE:

Be afraid. Be very afraid.

Sweet Clarion components handle the audio needs.

Greddy performance equipment covers the 2-liter engine.

2002 WRX Street Car

2002 **WRX Street Car**

To show off its extensive line of products, APC built a 2002 Subaru WRX for one of its show vehicles.

The exterior has APC carbon fiber front splitters, clear side indicators, Road Vision mirrors and Euro taillights. The 2.0-liter engine was left pretty much stock, aside from a Turbo XS blow-off valve, Blitz air filter, Nur spec exhaust and a Nitrous Express nitrous kit.

At all four corners are 18-inch Racing Hart CPO-35R rims wrapped in Falken FK451 rubber. The interior has Sparco Torino seats rewrapped in black leather and blue suede, and a custom roll cage.

Sound comes from a JVC head unit and Kicker Audio subwoofers, amplifiers and component speakers.

BOTTOM LINE:

So much fun, it comes with its own blood pressure gauge.

Kicker Audio subwoofers are wired to a JVC head unit.

The 2-liter engine received the nitrous treatment.

2000 Impreza Street Car

2000 **Impreza Street Car**

The WRX is by far the most popular Subaru in the tuner market, but Chris Duhain from Elk Grove, California, decided to take a 2000 Impreza 2.5 RS and create his own turbo Subaru.

The Impreza now has an AVO turbo system which utilizes a Garrett turbocharger, manual boost controller, intake, wastegate, blow-off valve, and top mount intercooler, Apex'I exhaust and Nology spark plug wires. All this spits out 325 horsepower at the wheels at only 6 psi.

Rolling stock are custom painted 17 x 8 Rays Super Turismo rims wrapped in Toyo T1-S rubber. A set of huge Brembo Gran Turismo drilled and slotted brakes are on duty. The exterior of the Subaru sports JDM clear corner lamps, STI grille, JDM side skirts and a Prodrive rear wing.

In the cockpit, Duhain opted for some Konig race seats, custom upholstery in the rear and door panels, HKS gauges, STI short shifter and Momo steering wheel. An Alpine in-dash monitor, DVD player, speakers, amplifiers, and Rockford Fosgate subwoofers provide the tunes.

Bottom Line:

More proof that aftermarket turbo kits are a wonderful thing.

JDM skirts and a Prodrive rear wing dress up the exterior.

The Garrett turbo is part of an impressive engine buildup.

1999 WRX Drag Car

1999 **WRX Drag Car**

Tony Rigoli Performance, or TRP, is known across the world as a great high-horsepower engine builder specializing in Subaru. At their shop in Sydney, Australia, the Rigolis took a 1999 Subaru WRX wagon and turned it into the world's fastest WRX. They have run a best time of 8.88 seconds @ 154.09 mph in the quarter mile.

The WRX engine is a 2.0-liter flat four that has been stroked to 2.5 liters and turbocharged with an Innovative T76 turbocharger. The engine runs eight 1200cc fuel injectors and three 800-hp Bosch fuel pumps. To aid the four-wheel-drive system off the line, a 100-hp Zex nitrous kit has been installed.

On a four-wheel Dyno, the WRX has been able to make 542 hp at the wheels at 7,500 rpm using 40 lbs. of boost and no nitrous.

Bottom Line:

A wagon with some sort of serious chromosome disorder.

A parachute and four racing slicks show this is a serious wagon.

A 100-hp nitrous kit helps this brilliant engine produce 542 hp.

Subaru

2002 WRX Drag Car

2002 **WRX Drag Car**

Ali Afshar is the owner and pilot of the world's fastest new-generation "street legal" Subaru WRX. Afshar is a six-time NHRA winner in the Sport RWD class. This WRX has gone 9.44 seconds @ 154 mph.

The car still boasts a full interior, glass and power windows, and fully stock metal body panels. His car still weighs in at 3,200 lbs. The power plant is a 2.5-liter engine making 950 hp. Power is created through a single GT72 ball bearing Innovative Turbochager. Ali's WRX has accomplished 1.89 0-60 times using a Subaru four-speed automatic transmission and runs BF Goodrich drag radial tires. Stopping the WRX are Brake Man front and rear "Storm" brakes.

For more information, see www.esxmotorsports.com.

BOTTOM LINE:

A 0-to-60 time of 1.89 seconds? In a street legal car? The cops'll be choking on their donuts.

It has license plates, but this Subaru belongs on the track.

The heart of this beast is a hairy 950-hp 2.5-liter engine.

2001 Lexus IS300 Turbo Street Car

2001 **Lexus IS300 Turbo Street Car**

Oscar Ramos's 2001 Lexus IS300 is a street car worthy of any road race track and has the performance to back up the great looks.

The original engine was pulled out and a Top Secret 3S-GE engine from Japan was installed. The 3S-GE engine was upgraded from stock status using a K-3 turbocharger, SARD fuel injectors, HKS head gasket, and a Blitz front-mount intercooler. An Ogura triple-plate clutch was installed to handle the extra power.

The exterior of the IS300 has a Top Secret front bumper, Wald side skirts, rear bumper, fender flares, and a carbon fiber hood and trunk lid. Ramos's wheel and tire selection includes 18 x 85-inch Volk CE37 rims with Toyo RA1 rubber. A Tein RH coilover suspension from Japan was brought in, and a Tom's nine-piece suspension brace kit was added.

A Top Secret steering wheel, Bride seats, Takata racing harnesses, and a Monkey Bars roll cage were all used to complete the interior. The audio system uses components from Alumapro, Zapco and Eclipse.

BOTTOM LINE:

Metallic gold paint and carbon fiber are sorta like food, water and air. We can't survive on this planet for long without them.

The Top Secret 3S-GE turbocharged engine has loads of power.

The carbon fiber trunk matches the hood.

1991 Toyota MR2 Widebody Street Car

1991 **Toyota MR2 Widebody Street Car**

Mark Cosio took his 1991 non-turbocharged Toyota MR2 and converted it into a high-revving turbo terror. The engine bay houses a Greddy TD06-SH turbocharger, HKS blow-off valve, Sport dual exhaust and a K&N air filter. Cosio also chrome plated virtually everything he could.

Inside the transmission is a Jun lightened flywheel and a Clutchmasters Stage 3 clutch. The suspension of choice for this MR2 includes JIC FLT-A2 coilovers, front strut tower bar and rear strut tower bar.

It all rolls on 18 x 9-inch Gram Light 57F pro rims in the front and 18 x 10-inch hoops in the rear wrapped with Pirelli P7000 tires.

In-car entertainment comes courtesy of Alpine Electronics, Infinity components, and a Kicker subwoofer. The cockpit has Bride Brix reclinable seats, Blitz gauges and diamond-cut floor mats.

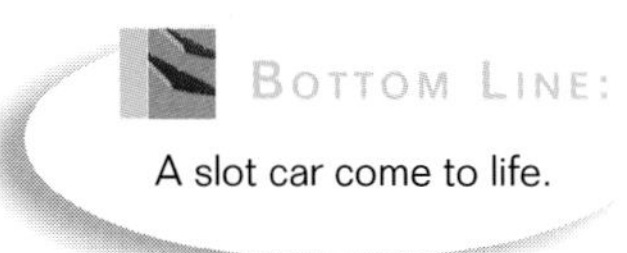

Fantastic interior upgrades bring this 1991 MR2 up to date.

The mid-engine design means the audio goes under the hood.

2000 Toyota MRS Street Car

2000 **Toyota MRS Street Car**

Alan Punsalan purchased this 2000 Toyota MRS knowing he was not going to just leave it stock.

Punsulan started off by installing an NOS 100-hp nitrous kit, Injen intake and Apex'I Power FC computer on the 1.8-liter engine. He then lowered the Toyota using Intrax springs and Tokico shocks.

For rolling stock, 18-inch Racing Hart C5 rims were covered with BF Goodrich tires. An APR GT2 carbon fiber wing and a body kit from West Coast spoilers finishes up the exterior nicely.

The interior is sharp with Momo NASCAR seats and race harnesses and Autometer gauges. The audio system has an Alpine head unit, JL Audio subwoofer, MB Quartz component speakers and a Kicker amplifier.

BOTTOM LINE:

Think about it; if you had one of these yellow dreams-come-true, what would you buy next? It'd be all downhill from there and your life would become hollow and without meaning.

This Toyoto received a complete makeover, including a widebody kit and wing.

Momo seats and Autometer gauges reside in an exotic interior.

2000 Toyota MRS Street Car

2000 **Toyota MRS Street Car**

APR built up this 2000 Toyota MRS to showcase its new products. The aerodynamics on the MRS include an APR S-GT widebody kit, GTC-300 carbon fiber wing, Formula GT3 carbon fiber mirrors, carbon fiber canards, custom carbon fiber wind splitter, a TRD hardtop, and a Fiber Images carbon fiber hood.

Utilizing TRD shocks, springs, stabilizers, front and rear strut bars, the MRS handles like a full-blown race car. The 18 x 8-inch and 18 x 10-inch Racing Hart C4 wheels are wrapped in Bridgestone S-03 tires to keep the car cornering well. Stoptech brakes were added for appropriate stopping power.

Power comes from a prototype TRD turbocharger, prototype exhaust system, and a Nitrous Express 50-hp nitrous kit.

In the cockpit, a pair of Recaro Pole Position seats keep the passengers planted on their back sides. A Momo steering wheel, Autometer gauges, Ignited push-button starter, and a custom carbon center console complete the interior.

The driver's seat is home to what looks like an airplane cockpit.

Carbon body parts are everywhere on this Toyota.

2001 Toyota MRS Street Car

2001 **Toyota MRS Street Car**

When you have a company like Apex'I and all its products at your disposal, you might tend to go a little nuts. That is exactly what Keith Imoto did.

Imoto works at Apex'I and when he purchased this 2001 Toyota MRS he knew it was going to become a crazy car very quickly. He started with a JDM TRD monocraft GT-300 widebody kit. Only 100 of these kits were built worldwide. On top of the MRS is a JDM OEM hardtop. A Varis carbon hood and carbon trunk lid took the place of the factory metal to complete the exterior.

To fit the widebody, 17 x 8-inch Volk Racing GT-P rims were mounted in the front with 18 x 9 rims in the rear. Toyo tires supply the traction. A massive 13-inch Rotora brake kit was installed to help slow the large wheels.

The 1ZZ-FE engine has an Apex'I AX53B60 ball bearing turbocharger kit fitted with a Power intake and side mount intercooler.

On the inside are Recaro seats, Takata race harnesses, and Momo steering wheel and shiftknob. The audio system thumps from custom enclosure and features JBL subwoofers, Kenwood monitor, Clarion DVD player, and Precision Power amplifiers.

Would be a dream to own, even if it never left the garage.

Without the JDM hardtop, this MRS is a truly wild roadster.

The heavy-duty audio is integrated behind the seats.

1997 Toyota Mark II Drift Car

1997 **Toyota Mark II Drift Car**

This spectacular 1997 Toyota Mark II is definitely no trailer queen show car. Weld Techniques Factory in Japan built this to not only showcase its products, but to show that a heavy show car with a full stereo system can be a drift car as well.

Sporting a fully built 3.0-liter 1JZ-GTE engine making 493 horsepower and 412 lbs.-ft. of torque, this car can turn and burn. The engine uses an Apex'I RX-6B turbocharger, turbo manifold and head gasket, Power FC computer, Sard 650cc fuel injectors, Fwin radiator, ATS twin carbon clutch, and a Weld exhaust system.

An Apex'I N1 coilover suspension handles a set of Work XSA wheels measuring 18 x 9 inches in the front and 18 x 10 inches in the rear. Bridgestone Potenza Re-01R tires are wrapped around the Work wheels.

The exterior of the Mark II sports a Weld carbon hood, T&E body kit and wide fenders, and Art Factory graphics. The interior is filled with a custom 14-point roll cage, Sparco steering wheel, Corsa seats, Sound OG Style dash panel, Weld engine starter, Apex'I gauges, Denon head unit and Kicker amps and speakers.

Bottom Line:

A fancy-schmancy show car that likes to get dirty and bloody.

Weld techniques didn't skimp on the paint and graphics.

The loaded interior is unique for a drift machine.

2003 Toyota Solara Drag Car

2003 **Toyota Solara Drag Car**

The MSP Toyota Solara owned by "the Greek" Efantis and driven by his son Paul is the fastest Modified Class car to date.

Powered by a 2JZ 3.0-liter inline six engine, the Solara has been able to run times of 7.42 seconds @ 185.79.

Internally, the 2JZ has Weisco Pistons, Carillo rods and HKS camshafts. Turbocharger selection for this vehicle is a Turbonetics T78 "Y2K". The transmission is a G Force GF 200 clutchless five-speed. The front brakes come from Strange Components, the back binders are from Wilwood. The back half of the Solara has a tube frame.

Bottom Line:

Look Dad, the front wheels come off the ground! How cool is that?!!

The front end gets light when Efantis hits the gas.

Huge performance has been wrung out of the inline six.

1997 Toyota Supra Widebody Street Car

1997 **Toyota Supra Widebody Street Car**

Bill Robards is simply crazy for Toyota Supras. He's owned four of these high-horsepower Toyotas, but the craziest is this 1997 hardtop twin-turbocharged machine.

Sporting more than 700 hp @ 6800 rpm with 1.85 bar of boost, the 2JZ 3.0-liter engine stock engine has been put on steroids. Twin HKS 2835 turbochargers, 264 cams, twin fuel pumps, 700cc fuel injectors, and—unbelievably—stock rods and pistons produce some serious power.

To keep that power to the ground, Robards relies on an HKS triple-plate clutch and an ACPT carbon fiber drive shaft. To fill the wheel wells of the widebody, humongous 18 x 11-inch Veilside Andrew F rims were used in the front, with 18 x 13-inch hoops in the rear. Pirelli P-Zero tires surround the monster rims.

Inside the cockpit is a 10,000 rpm TRD instrument cluster, Greddy gauges, Bride race seats, and a Momo Millennium steering wheel.

Just makes you wanna cruise around on a sunny Sunday with your arm out the window, doin' about 120.

Custom sheet metal gives this car a one-of-a-kind exterior.

Twin turbos help unleash more than 700 horses.

1993 Toyota Supra Widebody Street Car

1993 **Toyota Supra Widebody Street Car**

Bozz Performance took this Toyota Supra and made it a great replica of the Top Secret Toyota Supra from Japan. Using the Top Secret GT-300 widebody kit from Japan, Bozz was able to create a wild-looking JDM-style Supra.

Along with the widebody, a Top Secret carbon fiber hood and Cusco carbon fiber GT wing were added. The 3.0-liter 2JZ engine was ripped apart and reassembled with HKS rods, pistons, 272 camshafts, cam gears, GT2835 twin turbochargers, wastegate, and a Tanabe exhaust. All this makes for nearly 625 hp.

All that power would be useless without the OS Giken twin-plate clutch and Cusco MZ Type RS lSD. Cusco Comp L-Zero coilover suspension teamed up with 18 x 9.5-inch Volk TE37 rims on Yokohama Advan Neova tires.

Inside the Toyota, a Cusco six-point roll cage, Takata race harnesses, HKS gauges, and Bride seats all mean serious business. When you own a car like this there is no need for any audio system to compete with the sound of the turbochargers.

BOTTOM LINE:

Make sure you're strapped in when you hit the gas, or you'll wind up in the back seat.

The radical Top Secret body kit changed the look of this Supra.

Racing seats and harnesses are a necessity in a beast like this.

1994 Toyota Supra Street Car

1994 Toyota Supra Street Car

Ken Henderson owns one of the most interesting sleeper cars in the world. His 1994 Toyota Supra twin turbo looks from the outside like a lightly modified street car, but the horsepower coming out of the drivetrain of this understated beauty is downright scary.

A 3.4-liter HKS stroker motor produces an amazing 1,076 horsepower and 783 lbs.-ft. of torque at the wheels.

The Work Meister S2R wheels measure 18 x 9 inches in the front and 18 x 10 in the rear. They are wrapped in Bridgestone rubber. Behind the Work wheels are 14-inch Brembo cross drilled and vented brakes.

To complete the exterior, a Do-Luck type II body kit, type I rear over fenders, aluminum mesh grille inserts, 1997/1998 OEM headlights and turn signals, and a Philips 6000K HID headlight setup was all installed.

The interior is very simple. A plethora of Greddy gauges, Sparco Milano leather seats, Momo steering wheel, and HKS electronics round out the simple, clean theme.

Would fit right in as the next Bond-mobile.

This masterpiece is certainly one of top Supras on the street.

Few street cars can match this Supra's 1,076 hp and awesome torque.

1997 Toyota Supra Street Car

1997 **Toyota Supra Street Car**

There are definitely not many women in the tuner industry building or owning super high-performance cars. Lisa Uchida is an exception. She owns a super-hot 1997 Toyota Supra that turns plenty of heads.

The 3.0-liter 2JZ engine makes 610 hp and 520 lbs.-ft. or torque at 14 psi. To accomplish those numbers, HKS 272 cams, cam gears, T51R turbocharger, wastegate, Unorthodox Racing pullies, Fluidyne radiator, Veilside intake manifold, 100mm throttle body, and tons more HKS products were used.

The exterior of the car was left stock, with the exception of the MVP carbon fiber lip, to maintain some sleeper status. Toyo tires surround 18 x 8.5-inch Volk Racing SF Challenge rims up front and 18 x 9.5-inch wheels in the rear. An HKS Hiper damper coilover suspension was installed to lower the Supra.

A custom six-point chro moly roll cage was assembled inside to protect the driver. Recaro supplied the SP-G seats. HKS gauges fill the dash. The audio system includes an Alpine head unit, Soundstream and Alpine amplifiers, Boston Acoustics speakers, and JL Audio subwoofers.

Bottom Line:

Yup, a woman drives it. And nope, she's not taking you for a ride. Eat your heart out Skippy.

JL Audio subwoofers and an enourmous Soundstream amplifier fill the rear.

HKS gauges fill the dashboard.

1995 Toyota Supra Drag Car

1995 **Toyota Supra Drag Car**

Vinney Ten owns an insane 1995 Toyota Supra that makes more than 1,200 hp. Ten is an accomplished racer whose car was the first Supra to break the 12-, 11-, 10-, 9-, and 8-second barriers, and first Supra to break the 120-, 130-, 140-, 150-, and 160-mph barriers.

Ten is also the first engine builder to make over 1,000 hp in a Japanese engine without nitrous or alcohol.

His Supra has gone a best 7.66 seconds @ 177.18 mph. The engine runs an Innovative Turbo, 1,600cc RC Fuel Injectors, VTR Intake Manifold, and a VTR liquid-to-air intercooler. Internal engine parts include Carillo rods, JE pistons, and a stock crankshaft. His transmission of choice is a two-speed Powerglide.

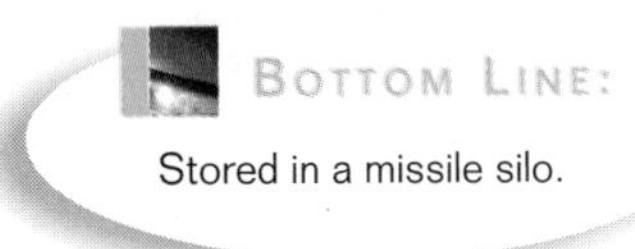

BOTTOM LINE:

Stored in a missile silo.

The wing, parachute and drag bars are all bolted to the back end.

Vinny Ten's Supra is a decorated race car.

2000 Golf Street Car

2000 **Golf Street Car**

This daily-driven 2000 VW Golf GLS has one of virtually everything that ATP performance offers, including intake manifold, downpipe, exhaust and front-mount intercooler. The 1.8-liter turbocharged engine has been upgraded with a K03-052 turbo, GIAC version 4 ECU and HKS blow-off valve.

Wendell's Volkswagen runs H&R coilover suspension with Bilsterin PSS rear Perches, Neuspeed front and rear sway bars and Neuspeed strut bar. Stopping power is supplied by an ECS Tunning Stage 4 Porsche front big brake kit and ECS Tuning stage 1R rear big brake kit. The Golf rolls on 19 x 8.5-inch BBS LM wheels with Toyo Proxes FZ4 tires.

Bottom Line:

A menacing little German destroyer.

Two 12-inch Infinity subwoofers are housed inside a custom enclosure.

Big wheels and brakes and a hot engine make this a killer VW.

2002 Beetle Drag Car

2002 **Beetle Drag Car**

The idea for a new Volkswagen Beetle roadster funnycar came from owner and driver Ronald Jutting of Ahlen, Germany. The carbon Kevlar body was designed and built in Germany.

The full tube-frame chassis was built at Bob Meyer Race Cars in El Cajon, California. The engine is a 3.0-liter Pauter Super Pro Engine mated to a two-speed Powerglide transmission. The engine is turbocharged by Innovative and runs Venolia pistons and Pauter internals. It's all good for 1,000 hp.

To help stop the Beetle, Strange Engineering carbon fiber disc brakes were intalled, along with twin parachutes.

Inside the driver's compartment, a hand-formed aluminum seat, Autopower race harness, and an aluminum butterfly steering wheel is all that is needed.

This car recorded a time 7.80 seconds @ 170 mph in its first pass.

Lotsa headroom, and it's silly fast, too.

Twin parachutes are on duty to slow this 1,000-hp rocket.

A full tube chassis and carbon Kevlar body make this Beetle a pure racer.

Index

Eddie Paul's Custom Bodywork Handbook

by Eddie Paul

Covers the latest customizing techniques in more than 200 dynamic color photos, and highlights 20 customizing projects involving everything from old school hot rods to today's hot tuner car models.

Get the look you're going for with instruction on:

- Frenching taillights
- Adding spoilers and aero kits
- Hiding door handles

Plus, much more!

Softcover • 8-1/4 x 10-7/8
176 pages • 200+ color photos
Item# **SGCBW** • $24.99

kp books
An Imprint of F+W Publications

700 East State Street • Iola, WI 54990-0001
715-445-2214 • 888-457-2873

Available from booksellers nationwide or directly from KP Books by calling: 800-258-0929

When ordering direct, please include $4 for shipping & handling to U.S. addresses, and sales tax for residents of the following states: CA, IA, IL, KS, NJ, PA, SD, TN, VA, WI. Non-U.S. addresses, please add $20.95 for shipping and handling.

1992 **Honda Civic Hatchback Drag Car**

Andrew Bermea of Deep Stage Motorsports located in San Antonio, Texas, owns and operates this 1992 Honda Civic Hot Rod class drag race car. Powered by a B18C1 twin-cam VTEC engine producing more than 700 horsepower, this Civic definitely has a ton of engine work going on.

Some of the power adders are AEBS sleeves, Ross pistons, Crower rods, 75mm throttle body, JG/Edelbrock intake manifold, and a very large turbocharger. To keep Andrew going straight down the track, Mark Williams axles, spool, brakes, and control arms were installed.

The car has run a 9.22-second quarter mile @ 158 mph.

BOTTOM LINE:

Is 1992 old enough to be considered "old school?" If so, this sizzling no-frills drag sled qualifies.

A simple cockpit setup is built for speed, not looks.

Wheelie bars and a parachute hint at this car's pedigree.

 1995 Honda Del Sol Drag Car